DAVID TAYLOR

HELL IN SINGAPORE

THE LOSS OF THE BLACKPOOL REGIMENT AND THE SINKING OF HMS YIN PING

David Taylor

DAVID TAYLOR

ISBN: 979-8-3563-7894-2

HELL IN SINGAPORE

DAVID TAYLOR

HELL IN SINGAPORE

iv

DAVID TAYLOR

DEDICATION

This book is dedicated with thanks to the

family of Alfred Burt Briggs.

CONTENTS

DAVID TAYLOR

ACKNOWLEDGMENTS

The extracts and quotations from Cary Owtram's book,
'A 1000 Days on the River Kwai', are reproduced with the kind
permission of Jean and Patricia Owtram.

Mike Coyle, author of 'The Blackpool Regiment' kindly allowed
me to use extracts from his work which is available at
fyldecoaster.wordpress.com

The drawing of *HMS Yin Ping* and all the maps are the brilliant
work of Alan Cavanagh, BSc, FRSA, FRGS.

My grateful thanks to the following, who have helped me in so
many ways: David Upton, Meg Parkes, Diane Seville, David
Maudsley, Stephen Boyle, Barry Band, Andrew Glynn, John
Muter, Christine Orme, Michael Pether and David Croft.

My special thanks to my assistant, Louise Morgan, without whose
help I could not have completed this book.

INTRODUCTION

This is the story of two ordinary men in war: one related to me, one known to me.

It is not concerned with the bold sweep of military tactics, battles, thrusts and counter thrusts.

It is not, in any way the full story of the 1941-42 Japanese campaign in Malaya, leading to the catastrophic surrender of Singapore, nor is it a complete military history of the 137 (Army) Field Regiment RA (TA), the Blackpool Regiment, as only brief outlines of the various engagements will be given.

Through the eyes of one particular individual, it tells the brief and tragic story of the Blackpool Regiment, founded and destroyed within three-and-a-half years. Shipped into a theatre of war in November 1941, the regiment was decimated in the battle of Slim River in January 1942, and never reformed. It was only in action for a mere nine weeks.

Some of those captured at Slim River were interned in Kuala Lumpur POW camp. Other survivors of the battle fought their way back to Singapore only to be forced to surrender. They were sent first to Changi POW camp and then from there to various other POW camps, mostly on the notorious Burma-Thai Railway, where many died.

I have tried to convey the constant movement of the whole sixty-nine day campaign: the continuous retreat, mostly through jungle, in desperately hot and humid conditions, pursued at all times by the relentless Japanese with little or no respite; the aching tiredness; the physical weariness; and the sheer terror they all must have felt.

Furthermore, it is not the full story of the RAF in Malaya at that time, as a full service history of its campaign is readily available.

In one case, I was kindly given access to private papers, and in the other, I have my own family knowledge to call on.

They are stories that anyone can relate to, to say 'that could have been me', and also to say 'thank God, it wasn't me'.

It is possible, though by no means certain, that the two men met prior to the fall of Singapore in February 1942.

At that time, Singapore was not a place for socialising – it was a place of bewilderment and terror, a place from which to escape, a place where law and order had broken down, where gangs roamed the streets and unrestrained looting prevailed amidst incessant shelling and bombing by the Japanese.

In telling the story of these two ordinary men, one must remember that attached to each would be the inevitable clutter of life – debts, obligations and worries – but also there would have been, especially at their ages, the laughter, the joy and the fun of life, all there to be preserved or lost in the conflict which lay ahead.

The men were Alfred Burt Briggs, whose war I will be following, and my mother's brother, Francis Ronald Emery, whose very brief sad time in Singapore I will be relating.

*****

I met Alfred Burt Briggs on several social occasions after the war. I was friends with his daughter Josephine, and he accompanied us to various dances as a rather unwilling chaperone. I also saw his picture many times in the local newspaper. He was one of the saviours of the Blackpool Grand Theatre when it was threatened with demolition. He was also involved in the local rugby club, Fylde, in Lytham St. Annes, where I was a player. He was a bank manager and very sociable. I would have been in my late teens or early twenties. He would have been in his fifties or sixties, so he passed in and out of my life, never really part of it, but always somewhere there in the background.

He died peacefully in his sleep in 2004. I wasn't aware of his actual death at the time and only heard about it later. I did not know then that he was, with countless others, a very brave man.

****

Manchester 1938. The Midland Hotel. Dinner-jacketed men. Ladies in elegant silk dresses. The sound of 1930s dance music.

The MC spoke, "My Lords, ladies and gentlemen, pray silence for Mr. J. F. Emery."

Mr. Emery, the local Conservative MP, rose to speak. At the end of the table sat Mr. Emery's son, my mother's brother – Francis Ronald, known as Ronnie. He was sitting contentedly, listening to his father, a large cigar in his hand.

It was the annual dinner of the Manchester Branch of the North West Cinematograph Exhibitors' Association. The great and the good of the local entertainment world were present and ready to enjoy themselves. Sidney and Cecil Bernstein, the future founders of Granada Television were there. Film stars Robert Young and Jessie Matthews were the guests of honour. It was a glittering and glamorous evening.

Of course, every small event is part of a larger scenario, itself part of a bigger picture and so on, linking, expanding.

A couple of hundred miles from Manchester, in London, while some cinemas were showing 'Three Comrades' – a strangely prescient post-World War 1 film with Robert Taylor and Margaret Sullavan and a script by F. Scott Fitzgerald – the government of Neville Chamberlain was contemplating the threat of Adolf Hitler, whilst Chamberlain himself was preparing for his trip to Munich.

There was an anxious restlessness, indeed fear, abroad everywhere that night. Europe in a ferment. Mussolini strutting. Jewish people terrified. The Sudetenland already annexed.

Further East, the British Empire (particularly India) was stretching and straining. Beyond that, as everyone was sitting down to a magnificent dinner in Manchester, the sun was rising in Japan on the plotters and the planners, staring intently at their maps of the Pacific.

Soon, my dear Uncle Ronnie would be caught up in events of which he had no control, and of which he had very little knowledge. In four years or so, he would be dead, killed in a war being fought on the other side of the world.

So, in London, Berlin, Rome and Tokyo, and indeed throughout the rest of the world, whilst the 16-piece orchestra in the Midland Hotel, Manchester, played 'These Foolish Things', and Ronnie danced contentedly with his fiancée, the second hand on the clock of fate was ticking inexorably away.

Poor Ronnie never stood a chance, and like most of those in the war which was to come he could never have possibly imagined his fate.

****

In 1938, Burt Briggs would also have been dancing. He would have been on his honeymoon with his beloved Isobel at the Hotel Belles Rives in Juan-les-Pins, in the south of France. He too would be caught up in life-changing events over which he had no control. Within four short years, he would be in a situation he could never have actually imagined.

PART ONE

THE BLACKPOOL REGIMENT

1. ALFRED BURT BRIGGS (BB)

The story of Burt Briggs is the story of every man in the 137 Field Regiment RA (TA) (known as the Blackpool Regiment), and probably the story of nearly everyone new to army service at that time.

All will have shared the absolute terror of being sent into battle. All will have wondered at the adequacy of the training. All will have been unimaginably hungry, tired and in great discomfort.

Alfred Burt Briggs, (I am going to call him BB hereafter) was born on 29th March 1912 at 31 Wood Road, Manchester, where his father was a talented photographer and the owner of several successful photographic shops.

His mother was Hilda Broadhead, whose father, William Henry Broadhead, established the theatrical chain which bore his name. He was born in Birmingham in 1849, but in order to improve his health he moved to Blackpool, where he happily immersed himself in the local affairs of his adopted town and became Mayor in 1905 and again in 1910.

He had two sons and four daughters, one of whom was Hilda (born 1886) who married Alfred Edward Briggs, a marriage which produced a son Alfred Burt Briggs (born 1912) and a daughter Hilary Briggs (born 1914).

The Broadhead Theatre Company, established by William Henry Broadhead and expanded by his two sons William and Percy, was based mainly in Manchester. The first acquisition was the Royal Osborne Theatre in Oldham Road, Manchester, in 1896. This was followed by a further 15 theatres, among them the Victorian Pavilion in Morecambe, the Empire in Ashton-Under-Lyne and the Crown in Eccles.

The Empire was especially luxurious and hosted some of the biggest names of the time, including George Formby Senior, George Formby Junior, Harry Houdini, Fred Karno (whose troupe included two young men destined for fame, Charlie Chaplin and Stan Laurel), Gracie Fields, and a very young Hylda Baker.

William Henry Broadhead died in 1931, his death causing great upheaval in the running of the company. The Empire was swiftly converted to a cinema and eventually sold to ABC. Closures and sales of the other theatres soon followed and within about a year of his death all the theatres had been sold off and the family theatrical chain consigned to distant memory.

In 1915, the family had moved to Blackpool where they lived on South Promenade. In the meantime, BB's father Alfred had been called up and was given embarkation leave before being sent to France in 1915.

Two years later, as a five-year-old, BB was sent to the High School in Blackpool, first as a day boy, but later on, when the war ended, he remained as a boarder because the family had moved back to Manchester.

The High School was founded in 1880 by Scotsman, A. H. Dolman M.A. and established, initially, in Alexandra Road, South Shore, Blackpool. In 1924, the then headmaster took a party of 15 boys from the High School to spend a whole month's vacation in Paris and to attend a course at the prestigious Sorbonne. BB was lucky enough to be included in the party. However, he does not seem to have profited greatly from the trip as he failed his final school exams. Grandfather William Henry Broadhead came to the rescue, and arranged for BB to go to Bromsgrove School, which he did in

1926, being driven there in his grandfather's splendid Daimler.

Bromsgrove was a well-known Church of England public school, officially established in 1553, although it is first mentioned in 1476 as a Chantry School, one richly endowed with land, goods and money. Many old Bromsgrovians fought and died in both World Wars. Some of them would have been contemporaries of BB, including Nigel Grey, a future recipient of the VC for his bravery in fighting the Italians in Ethiopia in 1945.

BB would also have been at Bromsgrove at the same time as the actor Richard Wattis, an actor best known for wearing thick-rimmed, round spectacles in British film comedies of the 1950s and 1960s.

His time at Bromsgrove seems to have been largely spent on the extensive playing fields. BB's housemaster had been a double blue at Oxford, and he encouraged BB in all sports, particularly Rugby Football. When BB left Bromsgrove in 1929, he did so as a fit young man, but not as one particularly well-endowed academically. Finding employment with limited academic qualifications was especially difficult in the 1920s, but BB was fortunate in that his father managed to find him a steady job, labouring at Rolls Royce Cranes Limited in Trafford Park Manchester.

Unfortunately, BB's parents decided that their marriage was over about this time and they went their separate ways. BB's mother nevertheless continued to enjoy her social life, happily representing her theatre-owning father at many social functions in Manchester, with BB accompanying her as her escort. She did not like to see his dirty hands from his work at Rolls Royce on these occasions, so again with the help of her father they secured a more 'respectable' job for him in Martins Bank in Manchester. He continued to work there until 1934 when the family moved back to Blackpool and BB was transferred to the St. Annes-on-Sea branch of Martins Bank.

His lifetime career, soon to be interrupted by the war, was established.

Such simple facts. How mundane. The story of thousands of

young boys of that age and at that time. Growing into manhood…finding a job…

Having become happily settled in Blackpool, BB immersed himself in the hectic social life of the area, and every year enthusiastically took part in the RAC Amateur Motor Rally, driving a variety of cars.

In 1936, his father was tragically killed in a motor accident near the Lake Windermere Ferry. BB had to abandon his holiday with Isobel Fielding – later to become his wife – to attend the funeral.

He had first met Isobel in 1935 at a tennis party at the home of her father, Joseph Fielding, a well-known Blackpool builder. The relationship flourished and on 30th April 1938 they were married at St. John's Church, Blackpool. Their luxury honeymoon followed in France.

Alfred Burt Briggs (BB)

2. FORMATION OF THE REGIMENT

Isobel's brother William was in the local TA Battery of the 88th Field Regiment, and he persuaded BB to volunteer. As well as knowing William, BB also knew Colonel George Dodgson Holme of the 88th Field Regiment, who happened to be the Treasurer of Fylde Rugby Union Club, where BB was one of the team secretaries. In April 1939, he persuaded some 15 other Fylde members to join the regiment with him and after a parade and an open day at the Yorkshire Street, Blackpool Headquarters, other local men joined. It took only 13 days for the regiment to reach its full complement of 548 men and 32 officers. BB himself was very conscious that his father had fought in and survived the 1914-18 War and he felt that he should keep the family flag flying.

There was tremendous pressure in Blackpool from the local Gazette, the Town Council and the Chief Constable E.H. Holmes.

All of them were pressing for a Blackpool 'Pals' Regiment to be formed as a separate unit.

Eventually, on 17th June 1939, the regiment was actually formed and became the 137 Field Regiment RA (TA), to be known as the Blackpool Regiment, with Lt. Col. George Holme RA (TA) confirmed as its first commanding officer.

BB was immediately promoted to sergeant, and invited to apply for a commission, which eventually came through in December 1939, war having been declared previously on September 3rd.

The 137 was a happy regiment. According to BB, "most of the men were locals from Blackpool and District and, in some cases, many of them were known to each other. The local officers shared the same connections. Other men were drafted in and became involved in the spirit of the regiment. It was always a very sound unit. Nearly 100 of the original members from Blackpool were eventually commissioned into the Royal Engineers in Singapore, the last one on February 13th 1942, two days before the surrender!"

In the late summer of 1939, the 137 Regiment went through an unsettling time as the 88th Regiment, Royal Artillery, (its parent Regular Unit) prepared to move to active service with the British Expeditionary Force (BEF) in France. Some of the younger soldiers of the 88th were exchanged for older members of the 137, which resulted in the regiment being left with a majority of young men, some of whom did not know the Blackpool area and had to travel to Blackpool for training.

Following the declaration of war, two initial artillery batteries were formed within the 137: the 350, based in Lancaster, and the 349, in Preston. A third battery, the 501, would be added on 3rd March 1941 prior to the regiment's departure to the Far East.

An artillery battery is the equivalent of a company, and is a separate unit of between six and 12 guns served by between 100 and 200 personnel, commanded by an officer.

For the first eight months of the War, the regiment was based in Blackpool, where all training took place. It was billeted in local houses or larger buildings. Some members were even billeted in their own homes. The regiment's civic duties included snow clearing around the Fylde area and helping to bring in the harvest, in addition to basic patrol and guard duties. Local entertainment centres and theatres regularly made their shows and dances available to the whole regiment for their enjoyment.

On May 1st 1940, nine days before the German invasion of the Low Countries, and while the BEF in France was preparing for that invasion, the main party of the 137 Regiment paraded at Blackpool North Shore Station before heading for Winsford Station in Cheshire, where they would disembark and march by road to the tented Oulton Park camp about six miles away.

349 Battery

However, the regiment was only in Oulton Park for just over a month, when, on June 5th 1940, it was ordered to Liverpool in anticipation of a German invasion. They were billeted in the grounds of Speke Airport and, before being moved to Knowsley Park, where training continued, albeit with some difficulty, as all the guns were of 1914-1918 vintage (or earlier) and had to be rebuilt.

BB later recalled how once, during this period in Liverpool, there had been extensive air raids and he described how his naturally chirpy demeanour was not always well received. After a night of relentless air activity, the following morning he was told to, "shut up Briggs!" by the CO, clearly irritated and frustrated by his sunny disposition and cheerful outlook.

Liverpool locals thought the regiment had been evacuated from Dunkirk and they were all looked upon as heroes, with plenty of free drinks on offer. Their heroism, of course, was to follow in the months ahead.

Eventually, in 1940, the regiment was moved from Knowsley Park to Larkhill in Wiltshire. The 349 Battery moved first, together with the regimental headquarters, with 350 and 501 Batteries following.

The move to Larkhill as the depot regiment was quite a high honour and the regular officers already in situ were amazed to find out that the new regiment was, in fact, a TA unit. The regulars were exceptionally impressed by the regiment's professionalism, its skill and its outstanding ability to perform set tasks, which it was always keen to demonstrate. This was clearly evidenced in April 1941, when King George VI and Queen Elizabeth visited the camp and saw a demonstration of a new way of laying down a quick barrage, which had been invented by 2nd Lt. Robert Hartley, a 137 officer, sadly destined to lose his life in Malaya. This method was eventually used at the battle of El Alamein with great success. According to BB, "the Royal visit was a high spot, together with the mounting of the guard with the Royal Artillery Band from Woolwich." He later recalled that he was "detailed to take the parade, presumably because of my loud voice, and I will always remember that wonderful occasion with pride." BB carried this vivid memory with him throughout his life. It was a clear indication of how much he valued being part of the 137.

Long after the war, BB discovered that the achievements of 137 as a depot regiment had not been properly listed on the Honours Board at Larkhill. Instead of acknowledging 137, it commended the 88th Field Regiment. BB said, "I proposed to take the matter up in due course, as I always found that there was a great deal of resentment about the fact that we were a TA regiment doing a regular regiment's job and doing it rather well in fact. They never forgave us for asking for a monthly mess accounting. The wine cellar was being stocked up at the expense of our rations, and that was stopped after I became Messing Officer."

A messing officer's duties included the promotion and management of all official functions, planning, menus and outgoings as well as the development and motivation of the catering team.

In addition, BB explained, "we gave a demonstration by one troop to Lt. General Alan Brooke, Commander in Chief Anti-

Aircraft Corps, and his accompanying senior members of staff. This troop had been given the task of helping to devise, within two weeks, a new method of air observation in conjunction with a Hurricane aircraft to replace the very much slower types used up to that time. I recollect that Major George Drought RA was the 349 battery commander at the time and his battery was designated to produce the answer, which they did."

On 27th September, the whole regiment entrained for a 12-hour journey to Liverpool, taking a circuitous route up the east coast, via Sheffield. Just three days later, after some 18 months' training, the regiment set sail from Liverpool on the 27,000-tonne luxury cruise liner, *Dominion Monarch*. BB said, "Blackpool Tower was the last thing I saw of England as it receded into the mist." He did not know that he would not see it again for another four years.

3. JOURNEY TO MALAYA

The *Dominion Monarch* was launched in 1939, and was the most powerful liner of its kind in the world at that time. Built on the River Tyne, she was certainly the largest ship operating full time to Australia. She accommodated 525 passengers (all first class) and 385 crew, and she held the record for the fastest voyage from Britain to Australia via the Cape of Good Hope.

***Dominion Monarch* (26,500 tons)**

On board this luxury ship there were many public rooms – the Palm Court, a large writing room, a restful drawing room, a grandiose old-world smoking room, with a Jacobean-style fireplace and mullioned windows, and a cinema. A delightful cocktail bar, something not normally found on passenger liners in those days, graced the port side. There was also the obligatory swimming pool, together with hairdressers and beauty salons, and more shops than one could mention.

The *Dominion Monarch* was at sea heading for Australia when war was declared on September 3rd 1939. The voyage continued to Sydney, where she was fitted with light armaments. She then continued her Australian service until August 1940, when she was requisitioned by the British Government. She was stripped of all her stylish and elegant fittings, painted grey and converted to a troopship capable of carrying 142 officers and 1,341 other ranks. The contrast with her former life could not have been more stark.

It was on this vessel, codenamed HMT B19, in convoy WS12 that BB, along with 1,672 troops and several nurses from the Queen Alexandra Nursing Service (189 more than the legal capacity), embarked on 29th September 1941. As well as the 137 Regiment, on board were also support units for the 11th Indian Division and some RAF personnel.

The *Dominion Monarch*'s armaments conversion must have been badly planned, as provision was made for only two guns: one salvaged from an 1899 Frigate, *HMS Venerable*, and the other, an ancient anti-aircraft gun, whose arc of fire had to be limited lest she fire at her own funnels!

On the journey, the 137 formed an entertainment committee and organised an elaborate concert party. They put on a two-night revue on 25th and 26th November entitled, 'I Remember'. By all accounts, it was a first-class production, with scenery, costumes and even wigs. More than 25 singers, musicians and other entertainers took to the stage, including Harry 'Ace' Connolly and his band, 'The Kings of Swing'. One of the band members, Bob Gale, wrote three original songs for the show, one of which was called 'Distance Makes no Difference', clearly a pertinent message for the time. Bob also appeared alongside his trio, 'The Rhythm Breakers'. In addition to the soldiers, a lone civilian (Mr Raymond) and four nurses all took their part on stage in sketches and imitations. Major Cary Owtram, second in command of the 137, gave a rousing rendition of 'Rose of England' and the penultimate song of the show was a patriotic number, 'Dominion's Parade', which showcased the theme of the whole show – the preservation of the Empire. It is unclear what role BB took in this theatrical extravaganza, but given his sociable, affable personality it is almost certain that he would have thoroughly enjoyed it, and would have immersed himself in the whole theatrical experience.

Lt. Col. G.D. Holme had been appointed the ship's military CO, and he detailed BB to be Messing Officer. According to BB, "this proved a useful occupation as the *Dominion Monarch* was still sailing under peacetime conditions with all the wonderful catering services of the pre-war cruising era. We were always supplied with beautiful sandwiches at whatever time we retired for the night. That time depended on the CO's musical memory and his prowess on the piano in accompanying his officers' rendering of mess songs. A good trip was had by all."

The regiment was all set for a jolly cruise, although occasionally rigid military discipline reared its ugly head. One officer later recalled that he was relaxing and sunning himself on deck, when he was ordered to take the pay parade, the duty pay officer being unwell. The pay parade was conducted shirtless, and without a cap, for which the officer was put on a charge, though it is not clear whether or not this was followed up.

The journey took them via Freetown in Sierra Leone, arriving on 14th October 1941, then Cape Town, where they had five days' leave, and then up to Colombo, where they had another extra couple of days' leave. The voyage continued via the Straits of Malacca to Singapore. The whole journey of some 14,487 U-boat-free nautical miles was enjoyed with all the careless abandon of a cruise at Government expense. And why not? For so many of the men and the nurses on that ship, it was the last sweet taste of freedom and enjoyment for three years. Tragically for some, their freedom was to be measured in only days or weeks.

The *Dominion Monarch* eventually arrived in Keppel Harbour, Singapore, on 28th November 1941, to be welcomed by a military band in full dress uniform playing martial music. Such pomp and ceremony seemed fitting for this grand ship and her passengers.

The regiment disembarked at 18:30 and immediately boarded three trains for Kajang, some 12 miles south-east of Kuala Lumpur and 220 miles from Singapore, reaching there at 06:30 on 29th November 1941. BB said, "on the journey all the officers were in first-class carriages, but were somewhat shattered by the change from the leisurely cruise to the jogging Malayan train."

If they, and the many troops arriving in Singapore almost daily, had had the time, they would have seen that the city in November 1941 appeared to be an exotic paradise. But as everyone knows, appearances can be deceptive. Over a number of years Singapore had developed from a swamp-covered island into a beautiful place following a deal made in 1819 by Sir Thomas Stamford Raffles, a far-sighted officer of the East India Company. He had negotiated a treaty with the local rulers and established Singapore as a successful trading station, attracting immigrants from the Malay Archipelago, India, China and beyond.

The population of Singapore at that time was about 600,000, consisting of between 50% to 60% Chinese, 30% Malayan and 10% Indian, together with a relatively small proportion of Europeans. The Chinese were mostly coolies and labourers.

It was at the crossroads of the trading routes between Australia and India, and South Africa and China. It became a fortified military base and home to the combined British Far Eastern fleet.

It was a paradise which, within three short months, was to be transformed into a hell.

Any wandering troops or tourists would have seen the beautiful central square named after Sir Stamford Raffles, which served as the hub of Singapore's commercial zone. They could not have missed the famous hotel bearing his name, opened in 1887 as a ten-roomed bungalow, and then expanded in 1899 to a three-storey building, including powered ceiling fans and electric lights. Famous past guests included Rudyard Kipling, Noël Coward, Joseph Conrad and Somerset Maugham. According to local legend, the latter wrote under a frangipani tree in the Palm Court every morning during his stay there, turning the snippets of scandal and gossip overheard nearby into his famous stories.

Throughout the town, there were many richly embellished religious buildings including the Sri Mariamman Temple, Singapore's oldest Hindu temple, which was finally completed in 1827, and St. Andrew's Cathedral, built over a five-year period, 1856-61, in the Neo-Gothic style. Also, well worth seeing was Chijmes (The Convent of the Holy Infant Jesus), a Neo-Classical private school. They could have visited the Fullerton Building, which had been commissioned in 1919 as part of the British colony's centennial celebrations. It was most certainly an ambitious project and the largest structure ever built in Singapore. It had 14 lifts and housed services and organisations such as the General Post Office, the Exchange, the Singapore Club, the Marine Department and the Import and Export Department. The Singapore Club was the only private-sector entity occupying space in the Fullerton Building in pre-war years and it was patronised by the 'well-heeled'. Additionally, they could have seen the Victoria Theatre, built in 1862, the concert hall built in 1905 and the National Museum on the Stamford Road.

To relax in the evening, the visiting troops could have gone to the new 1,300-seat cinema, situated on the ground floor of the art deco Cathay building, the first cinema in Singapore to be air conditioned and which was showing, to great acclaim, the 'Wizard of Oz'.

However, soldiers being soldiers, they would have preferred to go down to the docks and into the girlie bars, mostly run by the Chinese.

Almost certainly, they would not have had the time to pause by the War Memorial, located on the Esplanade, a memorial to the dead of World War One. If they had, shivers would have run up and down their spines. What would have been their thoughts? Would their names be on the next memorial? Sadly for many, that turned out to be true.

Newsreels of the time described Singapore as a "mighty guardian of the East", a guardian soon to surrender its duties. The city, the port and the harbour were all unconquerable and unassailable, or so it was thought.

However, the 137 Regiment had no time for sightseeing. On landing, they immediately unloaded, and marched to Singapore station. The temperature was warm but not overwhelming, at a modest 25C, although the humidity was an uncomfortable 80%. Monsoon-like rain was expected, but never materialised. There was still no sense of apprehension. The arrival at port, the disembarkation, the unloading and the march to the station were all undertaken in a spirit of joviality, with light-hearted humour and banter between all ranks. They may well have been well trained, but they had no idea what lay ahead.

'Ignorance is bliss'. Never was the phrase more appropriate.

More mundanely, on arrival, they would have been made aware of the dangers of mosquitoes. They were immediately ordered to adjust their uniforms, so that if possible, no skin was bare to the elements. Any uncovered parts had to be covered in cream. Sleeves had to be rolled down and fastened, and long trousers had to be worn at all times after sunset. For the members of the 137 such instructions were life-saving.

They boarded the train like a load of schoolboys on a day trip. They did not know where they were going or what they were going to do when they got there.

They knew nothing of Malaya, Singapore or the exotic East.

4. INTO ACTION

On November 30th 1941, the regiment arrived at Kajang, some 200 miles from Singapore, where they unloaded and were billeted in a school. Kajang was a small town in the province of Selangor. Its economy was based on tin mines and coffee plantations.

The first week was spent in settling in and sorting out laundry and other working arrangements, hiring dhobi wallahs to collect and launder clothes, in addition to every other type of servant that the Indian army could supply. Nobody seemed to be unduly worried about the war which was only a few days away.

BB said that, "on the surface, everybody was entertaining everybody else, rushing around and enjoying themselves. The question of war with the Japanese was rarely spoken about openly, but it was obvious that trouble was brewing." He added, "it was very comfortable after the 11 weeks' journey by sea in a troopship, but the eventual bombing of Singapore on 8th December 1941 put a stop to the kind of life we were living in Kajang, and we never rested again until 15th February 1942."

BB remembers a Brigade Major giving a lecture entitled, "This is what is going to happen when the Japanese attack".

He was proved correct in his forecast.

His opinion was that the plan to advance into Thailand to thwart any landings was 'pie in the sky', owing to the sparse number of troops available and the fact that there was very little air support. In fact, there were only 169 aircraft of all types in the whole of Malaya, and little or no liaison between the various services. Of course, everybody listened, but with varying degrees of concentration. In any event, what could they have done if they had accepted the talk at face value?

"Jolly good lecture, Sir!"

On 7th/8th December 1941, the Japanese invaded the Malay Peninsula, just a couple of hours before the attack on Pearl Harbor.

Soldiers from the 18th Japanese Division, supported by assault troops from 56th Infantry Regiment, and a mountain artillery battery landed on the narrow beaches of Badang and Pantai Sabak, 10 miles from the RAF airfield at Kota Bharu and some 450 miles from Singapore. The airfield was swiftly abandoned following the loss of five Lockheed Hudson bombers out of a total force of 10. The Japanese later claimed that the landings at Kota Bharu were some of the most violent and difficult of the whole Malayan campaign, losing 300 of their men killed, and 500 wounded.

Despite spirited resistance by the 8th Indian Infantry Brigade, supported by the 21st Mountain Battery and the 3/17th Battalion Dogra Regiment, the Japanese made extraordinary progress. Within three days they had reached the outskirts of Jitra, some 231 miles inland.

Rather belatedly, on the night of the 9th/10th December and two or three days after the Japanese invasion, the 137 Regiment had set off by road from Kajang to Jitra, (some 293 miles to the north) travelling via Ipoh and Sungei Siput, where, after a journey of between 12 and 15 hours, they joined the 11th Indian Division.

By this time, however, the Japanese were only 20 miles from Jitra.

Eventually, on 10th/11th December 1941, all three batteries took up position at the Tanjong Pau rubber estate covering the western part of the front, including the railway. Batteries 349 and 350 offered some protection to Jitra, whilst 501 tried to do the same for the Alor Star airfield.

BB said, "we were armed with 25 pounders, which were very

effective and were used with great effect. During my time on the railway, I met a Jap officer who had suffered from our 25 pounders at several places in the run down the peninsula, and he had quite a respect for the members of our regiment!"

The 25 pounder, designed in the 1930s, was the main field artillery weapon used by the British infantry. It combined the ability to provide both high-angle and direct-fire with quick-firing rates on a mobile platform. It was considered to be one of the best artillery pieces in use. BB's conversation with the Japanese officer confirmed this.

The frontline at Jitra had supposedly been specially constructed, but it was little more than a deep ditch, and the Japanese circumvented it by the simple device of going around it and attacking from the rear. Guns, having been securely well-positioned, had to be withdrawn in a great hurry. The action at Jitra lasted only a few days, but it was a complex and bitterly contested engagement in which BB and the 137 played only a relatively small part.

When it was clear that the Japanese were going to overrun the frontline from the rear, the order was given to withdraw. BB said, "the ammunition that we had loaded up into our limbers at Larkhill in September was actually fired at the Japs at Jitra on December 12th. It was a long way to carry high explosives."

Following the defeat at Jitra, Lieutenant General Arthur Percival, GOC Malaya, ordered all aircraft stationed in the Malayan peninsula to withdraw to Singapore.

So, that was it – BB and 137 Blackpool Regiment had been in action. They had tried to kill the Japanese, who in turn, had tried to kill them, possibly by long distance artillery fire or, after overrunning the battery positions from the rear, in face-to-face fighting.

It took only a few short months for the social life of "more tea, Vicar?" to become the brutal reality of "no thanks, there's a 25 pounder heading our way."

Could a mild-mannered bank clerk, accustomed to tennis parties, afternoon teas and social dances be suddenly transformed into a fighting soldier? Of course not. He would have been as petrified and bewildered as everyone else. How did he and his fellow soldiers cope? After all, just months before, and notwithstanding their training, none of them knew what war was all about.

Imagine yourself being spirited in an instant from your fireside and your loved ones, to a battle front and a conflict for which you had only minimal training.

According to veterans in more modern conflicts, war can be insanely exciting, exhilarating, vibrant and terrifying, subject to the infliction and receipt of terrible, physical and emotional injuries. A brotherhood of fighting men is the core experience of combat. The willingness to die for another person is a form of love, and is a profound and essential part of the war experience. Bravery is like greatness: one is either born with it or has it thrust upon one.

Royal artillery gunners kill at a distance, so BB might not have felt the adrenaline rush of combat. But he would certainly have felt it when confronted face to face with bayonet-wielding Japanese soldiers.

I, writing this book, and you, reading it, will almost certainly not have known, nor will ever know, the fear and the excitement of combat, recognising that any moment you might be wounded, perhaps mortally, or killed instantly.

Meanwhile, the Japanese smashed through the streets of Jitra without a shot being fired and with only nominal losses. Triumphantly, they captured the airfield at Alor Star, along with bombs and aviation fuel, both of which were subsequently used to attack the retreating British forces. Later, it was learned that the airfield had been abandoned without anyone being informed. In fact, it was abandoned so swiftly that the breakfast porridge was still simmering on the stove in the officers' mess as the Japanese took possession.

501 Battery, having assisted with the failed defence of Alor Star,

joined the 349 and 350 Batteries in the final defence of Jitra from the Tanjong Pau Rubber Estate, all in monsoon conditions, and all to no avail.

On December 14th, they were forced to withdraw in haste, abandoning their personal possessions in order to save the guns.

5. RETREAT FROM JITRA

137 Advance to Jitra and retreat to Singapore

The 137's retreat from Jitra took them 26 miles to Gurun, west of Pendang via the Jitra Road, a highway heavily congested with retreating troops, armaments and civilians. They counter-attacked on 15th December, but were eventually overrun. They were then ordered to withdraw south below the Muda River, leaving Battery 501 at Lalang, with instructions to re-join the regiment on 16th December at Bagai Serai, some 45 miles away. They marched mainly at night, to avoid daylight attacks.

According to a serving officer, "in the minds of all of us will live the memories of long night marches in convoy, when the fierce desire to sleep had to be fought with a mental tenacity greater than any called for by day; of the succeeding dawn when the drowsiness passed, leaving only the dull ache of tiredness; of the whistle of shells, all of which were alarming at first, though we later learned to distinguish those which fell at a safe distance; of the steady hum of circling planes, the louder roar as they dived, the rush of the bomb and the tense moment of uncertainty before it hit the ground."

He described how, "the night marches were our sorest trial. They were the reality of Japanese superiority in the air. While the planes wheeled overhead we could not move without risk. We moved by night. We fought by day. In our impotence we watched the Japanese airmen searching for their target, coming closer to make doubly sure, then diving to the attack. There was a rattle of small arms fire and somewhere behind the pom-pom-pom of a Bofors: but always the planes soared away undamaged."

According to BB, "during the retreat down the peninsula from Jitra, we supported the depleted infantry in many rear-guard actions. Our CO George Holme became an expert motor-cycle rider. At the Sungei Muda River he was in charge of the rear party of the retreat and having reconnoitred the most obvious spots for crossing the river, he was able to bring fire down on the Japanese for some three to four days, thus preventing them crossing and enabling the division to regroup before withdrawal to join them.

It was here that he was able to form a composite battalion of infantry under Captain Freddie Thompson of the Leicesters from men who had been cut off by the Japs at Jitra. This became known as the British Battalion and was eventually composed of Surreys, Leicesters, Royal Marines and Naval ratings from the *Prince of Wales* and *Repulse* sunk early in the campaign." He related how, "we were many times strafed from the air by Jap planes, and as our air force was non-existent the Japs had it all their own way. They often flew at a few hundred feet throwing out grenades as well as dropping bombs."

On 15th/16th December, Gurun was overrun and although the 501 Battery was in action at the Heawood Rubber Plantation, it was still forced to retreat.

Over the next five days, up to 21st December, 137's withdrawal continued some 53 miles from Bagan Serai to Sungei Siput, and a further nine miles from Sungei Siput to Chemor, where they rested.

By 23rd December, the regiment had resumed their withdrawal south towards Tasek, approximately five miles away. In this part of the journey, the 501 suffered casualties of four dead, six wounded and the loss of two vehicles as a result of dive-bombing by Japanese planes.

En route, down the peninsula, just north of Ipoh near Chemor, the regiment spent a relatively quiet Christmas Eve and Christmas Day. No doubt all the men were thinking about their families at home, serving men and families celebrating Christmas in very different ways.

BB later told the story of how, "we stationed ourselves in a planter's bungalow, just off the road. It was left just as though the owners had gone out for a drink. The staff were still about and the Chinese boy welcomed RHQ and we settled in for Christmas. We had three days here and our CO George Holme was called upon to carve the chickens that had appeared. A very good substitute for Christmas pudding was produced by the officers' mess cook."

He continued, "We were visited by some of the officers of the three batteries and we wished each other well for the future. A visit to the abandoned NAAFI in Ipoh by the Quartermaster produced replenishment for our rations lost in Jitra, and enough cigarettes to last the regiment for the rest of the campaign."

The enemy was spotted on 26th December, and a five-hour concentration of fire on each of the Japanese positions followed. The onslaught, however, was not enough to stem the relentless Japanese advance. Two days later, the regiment were reluctantly forced to retreat again, this time to Dipang 24 miles away, where the marching columns were dive bombed and machine gunned, five men being wounded.

On 29th December, 501 Battery moved a further five miles to Kampar, where they were joined shortly afterwards by the rest of the regiment, including the RHQ.

BB later recalled how, "In a hide just off the road, we were having breakfast in a planter's bungalow and on the receiving end of a couple of Jap zeros (single-seat low-wing monoplanes). We dived under the floorboards only to surface later to find the CO eating his breakfast and remarking that he did not like cold bacon and eggs."

At Kampar, from 30th December 1941 to 2nd January 1942, the 137 were embroiled in a four-day vicious battle, notable for the effectiveness of the British artillery, and where the Japanese suffered heavy casualties.

It was clear, however, that as the regiment retreated to the Bikan-Sunkai area, panic set in as the last entry in the regimental diary was 31st December 1941, which also happened to be Second Lieutenant Hartley's 30th birthday.

By 2nd January 1942, the 11th Indian Infantry Division, of which 137 was an important unit, had been outflanked by seaborne landings south of Kampar, and the road to Singapore had been cut off behind them. They were outnumbered, and with the Japanese attempting to cut the division off from the only road to Singapore, the 137 withdrew through almost impenetrable jungle to Trolak, five miles north of Slim River, and approximately 40 miles from Kampar.

A Japanese officer described being in the jungle as "ferociously sultry. The effect of dense thickets is like shutting the door in one's room. If you stay inside for long you develop a headache. Drifts of fallen leaves make walking difficult, your head and arms keep getting caught up in twisting branches, your cap keeps being knocked off, your skin scratched. There are no wild animals, but plenty of snakes and lizards. We see occasional crocodiles in the river and there are masses of centipedes and scorpions."

The heat and humidity would have been particularly draining for the soldiers of the 137, men much more used to the damp Lancashire climate.

The retreat to Trolak is described by Harold Payne, an officer in the 137 in his Imperial War Museum recorded interview. He recalls the "humiliation" of Japan's complete air superiority. Men and vehicles were "sitting targets" on the single road. The men could take cover in the jungle, but not with their heavy guns and vehicles. The Japanese infantry were in hot pursuit. Mortar bombs were falling all around – it was "a nasty experience". The men weren't sure whether people in paddy fields were Malays or Japanese. Some appeared to be helping the enemy with bamboo stakes pointing to the British positions. He concluded in his typical matter of fact style, "we shot them. That's war".

Payne recalls that the "most degrading" aspect of the campaign was the "total lack of air support". He describes the yellow paint of the British guns and vehicles as "stupid", making them highly visible to the Japanese airmen. This was because the equipment had initially been painted for desert warfare and not for action in the jungle.

At Trolak, the 350 Battery Commander heard that Japanese tanks had broken through the lines of defence. He ordered them to retreat towards Slim River, three miles to the south. But before the retreat began, the guns – the precious guns – transported all the way from Larkhill, to arrive in Trolak, via Singapore and Jitra, had to be spiked, which was "a terrible thing for an officer to do".

The 350 Battery then withdrew very quickly, bypassing the

Cluny Estate, where 349 and 501 Batteries were stationed, without being aware that the two batteries were actually dug in there. However, those batteries were not missed by the pursuing Japanese light tanks which discovered them breakfasting by the roadside. They were caught completely off-guard and were shelled, suffering a high number of casualties.

When Colonel Holme, who was with 350 Battery, was told about the Cluny rubber plantation disaster, he insisted on going back to help. He dashed off on a motorcycle, but sadly he was never seen again. Apparently, he ran into patrolling tanks and was shot dead. BB said, "After the war, it was discovered that he had been buried at Taiping War Cemetery, but I do not know how he got there as it was many years after the war that we were able to confirm his burial place. Perhaps all the graves from the retreat were moved to one central point." Major Cary Owtram, Second in Command, commended him as "a very brave and able soldier."

On 7th January 1942, half a dozen small Japanese tanks and 100 infantry reached Slim River. The bridge across the river had been wired for demolition, but the speed of the Japanese advance was such that a Japanese officer (Lieutenant Watanabe) was able to jump out of the tank and, with his sword, sever the fuse to the British demolition charges. In a curious twist of fate later in the war, BB recognised Lieutenant Watanabe at Tarsau POW camp in 1943.

Between 150 and 200 men of the 137 Regiment, (mainly, 349 and 501 Batteries) managed to survive the Slim River battle, the remainder (some 273 officers and men) having been killed, captured, or missing in action. The survivors decided to try and regain the British line at Kuala Lumpur, about 50 miles to the south. They split into two parties, but one party was quickly captured.

The other party, led by Major Cary Owtram, including BB, crossed the Slim River over the damaged railway bridge. BB said, "I held the rope for everybody to go across and then, somehow or other, the rope got entangled in something else and I was left on the wrong side of the river. Just at that moment a Gurkha battalion arrived on the scene and the Gurkha officer in charge was a very little man – although he wasn't a Gurkha, he was a Britisher. He looked at the river and decided which way was safe to cross for his small soldiers. So I followed them, and crossed the river without any trouble, got on to the railway line and marched off with the rest of what was left of the regiment towards Tanjong Malim."

According to Harold Payne, the survivors then trekked through jungle and formed human chains to get across the rivers. He said, "it was a choice between crocodiles and Japs". They could not shoot the crocodiles for fear of being heard, so they threw rocks at them. Payne remembers being, "tail-end Charlie" during one hand-holding river crossing. This story gives us a glimpse of the fear which must have been present during this perilous part of the journey. Being at the end of the line made him extremely vulnerable. How many times had BB also experienced similar feelings? How many times had he, too, been 'tail-end Charlie'?

They were on the move in the jungle, from around midday on 7th January until 9th January 1942, during which they probably made no more progress than three miles a day in daylight. During the night, however, marching on the railway line, and no doubt after a brief sleep beside the track, they may have made 15 miles. BB recalls wading across the river at Slim Station, where the railway and the road met. The tricky terrain and the unpredictable currents and sheer fatigue must have made the journey utterly exhausting for them all.

They reached Tanjong Malim on the morning of 8th January 1942, where they met an Australian transport unit, which took them 40 miles to Batu Caves, on the northern outskirts of Kuala Lumpur, where they had hoped to find a "British line". But that was unfortunately non-existent.

Forty-eight hours later, in the early hours of 10th January 1942, they walked into the centre of Kuala Lumpur, where a very senior British general, on a fact-finding visit from Singapore, rebuked them, yelling, "you men look disgraceful. Smarten yourselves up!" Apparently, the response from the men was unrepeatable!

According to BB, in typically British fashion, "we (the officers) were all admitted to the Selangor Club, or Spotted Dog I think it was called, in Kuala Lumpur, and as usual in those days signed chitties for everything including our membership fees and two or three nights' revelry. But the Japs moved too rapidly down the peninsula, overtook the post and ourselves, and we never received any bills for anything whilst in Malaya or Singapore. It was the cheapest, most unusual holiday I have ever had in my life!"

At Kuala Lumpur, the remaining men of the three batteries again separated. 350 Battery was re-equipped, attached to 155 Field Regiment RA and moved to Malacca to guard the retreat of the Indian, Australian and British troops heading for Singapore. In desperation, the remnants of 349 and 501 Batteries, the survivors of Jitra, Kampar and Slim River (including BB), fell on to what was probably the last train to Singapore.

By this point, they had been in action for a whole month, with no air cover and in monsoon jungle conditions, for which they had not been trained. They had lost all their personal possessions and their guns had been spiked.

At Tebong, 80 miles from Kuala Lumpur, the level crossing gates were closed and the train was forced to stop. In retrospect, BB believed that a Japanese agent had arranged for the level crossing to be closed to facilitate the ensuing air attack by Navy Mitsubishi Zeros.

BB said, "when we got to a place called Tebong, we were attacked by Japanese planes. They bombed the train, knocked the carriages about, broke all the glass and we were all in these beautiful train carriages with air-conditioning and everything else which, of course, was destroyed. Most of us, I think, were in the nude because that's how you sleep out there – without messing about. And we got out of the train when the planes had gone, hid ourselves in the palm trees at the side when the second wave came in and bombed the station and killed about three or four officers and about 10 or so troops. At any rate, we re-boarded the train, having got ourselves properly dressed, but the driver refused to move any further. He was a local Malayan native and was off home. So, we rallied the troops until we eventually found another driver. We set off again and the train was driven all the way to Singapore, where we detrained and where we were armed with 75 millimetre 1914-1918 war guns from the ordnance there and put in special positions to fight the Japanese when they came. Needless to say, that didn't happen, as it didn't go on for very long because on 15th February we all capitulated."

He continued, "the train was always under attack. Bombs. Planes used to come over in broad daylight – twenty-seven at a time. Three formations of nine, and they would just come over and drop all the bombs together hoping for the best."

The attack on the train had killed an unknown number of civilians, and 10 soldiers, among whom was 2nd Lt. Robert Hartley. According to Harold Payne, who was in the next carriage, he was killed in a direct hit on the train and was buried near there by "the other lads from Blackpool". Those lads from the Fylde would have found it so hard to bury their own. Of course, it could have been BB as he was also very close to the carriage where 30 year-old Hartley lost his life.

Harold Payne reported the death at Tebong Police Station. He said that when the train was about to be attacked, he saw all the natives running around in panic. He thought they looked as if they had disturbed a wasp's nest.

The restarted train covered the remaining 155 miles to Singapore without incident, arriving there on the 12th January 1942.

6. THE SURRENDER

On arrival in Singapore, the survivors of 350 Battery had been transferred to its parent regiment, the 88th Field Regiment RA, along with the survivors of the train journey from Kuala Lumpur.

On the night of February 7th/8th, a further transfer to the 5th Field Regiment took place. They were moved to work on Singapore Island near the Jurong River, where an attempted Japanese landing was repelled.

On February 12th, all forces were ordered back to a perimeter surrounding the city. Eventually they were allocated some old French 75 mm guns, which they set up outside Raffles Hotel and the Vicarage, engaging the enemy whenever they could, sometimes fighting with their backs to the sea.

This limited resistance lasted from the time of their arrival in Singapore on 12th January up to the time of the eventual surrender, just over a month later.

On 2nd February 1942, a special order had come from General Sir A.P. Wavell as follows: *"The Japanese are straining every nerve to keep the advantage gained by their initial treacherous surprise and to gain quick success. Once the impetus is halted they will soon lose courage. Our task is to check them and to gain time for the great reinforcements which we and our American allies are sending to the eastern theatre of war. We are in a similar position to the original*

BEF, which stopped the Germans and saved Europe at the first battle of Ypres. We must show ourselves worthy successors of them and save Asia by halting the Japanese.

We have now reached an area where we cannot be constantly outflanked, and where the enemy cannot exploit his superior mobility. We must yield no foot of ground without fighting hard and leave nothing behind undestroyed that could be the least use to the enemy. Our friends and allies the Dutch are carrying out the policy in every part of the Netherlands East Indies with superb sacrifice and resolution.

I look to you all to fight this battle without further thought of retreat, and to make the defence of Singapore as remarkable and successful an exploit as the defence of Tobruk, which British, Australian and Indian troops held so long and so gallantly."

However, at 8:30pm, on 8th February 1942, whilst the cocktail bar at Raffles was still serving Singapore Slings, and the pianist was playing Cole Porter tunes, General Yamashita's troops crossed the narrow waterway on the virtually undefended west side of Singapore. Unfortunately, the invasion had been expected in the north, where most of the protecting forces were stationed.

Lieutenant General Percival was in overall command and he had been instructed by Churchill that there was to be no thought of surrender until there was protracted fighting among the ruins of the city. He had 85,000 men under his control, of which 70,000 were combat troops. By contrast, the Japanese had only 30,000 combat troops.

However, by midnight on 8th February, 1,000 Japanese troops were securely ashore, and the defending forces were already in retreat to the Jura Line, a fall-back position, only a few miles away. The Jura Line's defences were ineffectual and they fell to the Japanese on 10th February. At the same time, the Japanese were also landing in the north as originally anticipated.

On the same day, Field Marshall Wavell issued the following: *"It is certain that our troops on Singapore Island heavily outnumber any Japanese who have crossed the Straits. We must destroy them. Our fighting reputation is at stake and the honour of the British Empire...It will be disgraceful if we yield our boasted fortress of Singapore to inferior enemy forces...Every unit must fight it out to the end and in close contact with the enemy."* He continued: *"It will be a lasting disgrace if we are defeated by an army of 'Clever Gangsters' many times inferior to our own...There must be no thought of further withdrawal without orders..."*

On 11th February, the area around Bukit Timah Hill, Singapore's tallest hill at 163 metres, and a mere eight miles from the city centre, fell when a counterattack failed. It gave an excellent view of the city of Singapore, enabling the Japanese gunners to inflict terrible damage at will. The next day, the three reservoirs serving the city were captured, thus cutting off the main water supply.

February 13th 1942 was pivotal. The Allied troops withdrew further to defend the actual city centre of Singapore, and whilst all ships were ordered to leave the harbour, and head for Java and Sumatra, for various reasons some were delayed and unable to depart as ordered. On the following day, the Japanese troops reached the Alexandra Hospital. A doctor carrying a white flag of surrender was bayonetted to death. There followed an orgy of killing with more than 100 patients, some of whom were actually on the operating tables, nurses and doctors being bayonetted or shot. Both the living and the dead were looted. Any survivors were locked up overnight without food or ventilation and then executed the next day. Two wounded members of the 137 were amongst those who lost their lives.

Yamashita's motive for this massacre was to show Percival that an utterly mindless and totally ruthless force would be unleashed on the citizens of Singapore if he persisted in ignoring his demands to surrender. In reality, this was a huge bluff on Yamashita's part. He knew that the Japanese had run so low on ammunition that they had only three rounds of artillery shells left for each of their guns, and he was well aware that his infantry was about to run out of ammunition altogether. The bluff forced the surrender.

Indeed, the situation was beyond saving, and at 4:15pm, on 15th

February 1942, at the Ford Motor factory at Bukit Timah, the instruments of surrender were signed.

At 8:30pm, 80,000 troops in Singapore and 50,000 elsewhere (if not already captured), laid down their arms and surrendered. According to Express Newspapers, Singapore had fallen to "a band of ugly little yellow men with protruding teeth".

General Percival's order on capitulation on the 15th of February 1942 was as follows: *"It has been necessary to give up the struggle. But I want the reason explained to all ranks. The forward troops continue to hold their ground, but the essentials of war have run short. In a few days, we shall have neither petrol nor food. Many types of ammunition are short, and the water supply on which the vast population and many of the fighting troops are dependent threatens to fail. The situation has been partly brought about by hostile aircraft and military action. Without the sinews of war, we cannot fight on. I thank all ranks for their efforts throughout the campaign."*

Having surrendered, BB said, "the Japanese didn't know what to do with us. So they looked at the map, and decided they would march us all into Changi, which is, as you know, the little bit that juts out on the east corner of Singapore Island."

Changi was about 12 miles from Singapore City Centre. The troops, on their enforced march to Changi, had to endure the humiliation of marching through the streets of Singapore in front of most of the civilian population, who could not show any sympathy for fear of reprisal by the Japanese soldiers who lined the route, and who were, in some cases, not as tall as the rifles they carried. Out of the city, they marched through swamps and forests, native villages, and coconut and rubber plantations. The parade of weary and exhausted soldiers, "a dirty, thirsty, sweaty, demoralised herd of losers", according to Ronald Searle, an artist and satirical cartoonist, and future creator of St. Trinian's School, appeared to go on forever. There were thousands of men in overwhelming numbers. How was it possible that they had lost the fight and were forced to surrender? To add to the humiliation they were made to hand over watches, rings and other personal possessions to the grinning Japanese guards.

Approximately 41,500 men arrived at Changi army camp on the first day, followed on the next day by another 10,700. The survivors arrived at an almost exotic place where there were four new three-storey barracks set in parkland, with adjoining married quarters, churches, theatres, cinemas, sporting facilities including squash and tennis courts and, of course, swimming pools.

The Australians were housed in the Selarang Barracks, with the British in the Roberts, India and Kitchener Barracks. The sick and wounded were placed in the Roberts Hospital.

The remnants of the 137 were, for a time, billeted in Roberts Barracks, where, before the War, all British troops had been quartered.

So what was the overall position of the Blackpool regiment, the 137, at the time of surrender on 15th February 1942?

Do not forget that the regiment had been divided following the battle at Slim River, part of the regiment 'escaping' to Singapore, and the remainder fighting on in the Kuala Lumpur area, eventually being killed, captured or amalgamated with another regiment. Even before the Slim River battle, following the collapse at Trolak, no actual record of the 137 as a unit existed so one is forced to rely on the memoirs of BB and others

In fact, the surviving parts of the regiment were not to be reunited until well after the surrender, when they were all in POW camps. BB, of course, was in that part of the regiment now divided into two batteries, which eventually made it to Singapore, participating in the regiment's historic last stand before surrender and capture.

It has already been related how the survivors of the regiment were marched off to Changi. Before they started on that march, they were forced into the humiliation of having to line the route of the Imperial Japanese Army's victory parade.

In Changi, the survivors of the regiment were confirmed in their two batteries, each with a full structure of officers, NCOs and serving men.

Jobs, such as cleaning and fixing the latrines, repairing the cookhouses and generally restoring any bomb-damaged buildings were ordered to be undertaken.

They remained in the Roberts Barracks for only about a week, when the Japanese decided to move some of the military prisoners to Changi Gaol itself, which was about two miles away. Changi Gaol was formerly a civilian incarceration unit but was now solely for POWs.

For some reason, it appears that BB and his regiment were treated differently, as they were housed in huts, bungalows or tents. It is not clear why. Perhaps they were just in an overflow situation.

BB said, "We went there and lived for two days in an old army hut and then we were told to move out to a bungalow at a place called Loyang – I think it was – and this bungalow, one of several, on the Johore Straits was quite comfortable and we lived there for several days." Loyang was a kampong or village on the east coast of Singapore, adjacent to Changi village and the army camp, where the POW camp was established.

BB was asked if the officers were living separately from the men. He replied, "Yes. We had the bungalow and the men were in tents in the grounds. What little there was of them, because of course half the regiment got caught up at Slim River and finished in Kuala Lumpur Camp. We didn't see them until later. So there was one part of the regiment back in Singapore, and the remainder of the regiment were up somewhere in Malaya, as far as we knew. Of course, it wasn't until many months afterwards that we found out where they were and what had happened to them."

The bungalows were well equipped with furniture and books. In one of the bungalows there was a generator which was quickly made operational. This bungalow was used as the officers' quarters and mess.

The Japanese were so impressed with the fact that the electricity was working, that they allowed continued use of the electricity generators, provided their headquarters were similarly wired up.

Very shortly afterwards, however, the 137 POWs were moved to Birdwood Camp just outside Changi as part of the 11th Indian Division, where they were ordered to create a fence that would, in fact, wire themselves in.

In Birdwood, they were guarded by Sikhs, who had defected to the Japanese in order to serve in the Indian Free Army on a promise that eventually they would be liberated from the constraints of British rule and the British Empire. In this they were destined to be disappointed, but whilst they acted as guards they were sometimes as cruel as the Japanese.

The work parties from Birdwood were either standard details going out of the camp each day to a particular task and returning every evening, or longer-term details where prisoners stayed away from the camps for some time, salvaging vehicles, building and repairing roads and airfields, or working in the docks.

It was estimated that up to 10,000 allied prisoners, including some from the 137, were living in Singapore or the suburbs on permanent work. Birdwood Camp was very different in comfort terms from the bungalows at Loyang, but under the command of Major General Billy Kelly the whole camp, 3,000 prisoners in all, became organised. Gardens were dug, sports teams (football, cricket, rugby) formed, and concerts and lectures arranged.

There were both Church of England and Roman Catholic clergy and services, including Communion.

One of the many problems (apart from the fact of incarceration itself) was the food. For a time, everyone was able to subsist on the surviving stock of army rations, and a weekly delivery of "European" food, which the Japanese brought up from various cold-storage depots in Singapore.

However these supplies rapidly dwindled, and the Japanese decided that all prisoners should learn to eat rice. Meat and flour were no longer part of the daily diet. The Army cooks did not know how to prepare rice, and so it was usually a soggy mess, flavoured occasionally with sardines, jam or curry, indeed anything to disguise the taste.

Inevitably, severe diarrhoea was the consequence of the change in diet. As the latrines were disgusting, and despite all efforts to keep them clean, dysentery followed the diarrhoea. The sufferers were taken to Roberts Hospital, where, if they did not die, they had to follow a strict regime of starvation plus Epsom Salts three times a day. This could be a cure, though one could lose as much as four stone in a fortnight.

Early in March 1942, the Japanese ordered a working party of prisoners (including BB) to be moved to Kranji Camp, about 10 miles from Changi. This was to be their base while they helped build a Japanese war memorial on top of Bukit Timah Hill, the site of the Ford Motor factory where the surrender took place. In order to achieve this, the working party in effect had to remove the top of the hill and dispose of the debris from the excavation in small wicker baskets.

Kranji Camp was a former Fleet Air Arm camp, untouched by the Japanese since the surrender, but looted by locals.

BB was again appointed camp messing officer. Through an interpreter he was asked by a Japanese officer whether he knew anything about electricity. BB certainly did not, but he found someone who had sufficient knowledge to wire up the camp's electricity. The electricity mains were in a hut in which there were rows and rows of boxes, all containing radio valves.

BB arranged for the valves to conveniently vanish. They were then concealed in drums of petroleum jelly which had been found in the Ford works, which formerly occupied premises on Bukit Timah Hill. In these containers, they were transported back to Changi by the unknowing Japanese. The valves were then distributed and used by the POWs in the manufacture of water bottle radio sets, which were utilised in various POW camps for the rest of the war.

Eventually, orders were given that the 137 survivors, plus others, totalling some 3,000 men, should prepare to be moved to an unknown destination.

Lieutenant Colonel Eddie Gill was placed in charge of the 137 survivors (some 330 in all) because the Camp Commander Lieutenant Colonel Cary Owtram was too ill to travel. He would rejoin his regiment later.

The rail journey was a nightmare, 1,150 miles in all. Between 25 and 30 POWs occupied each steel cattle wagon, with no bedding or toilet facilities. The Japanese provided two identical meals per day, consisting of rice and watery stew. The first stop was Johore Barhu, where local Tamils and Chinese crowded the platforms, selling or giving away eggs, fruit or bread. This pattern was repeated at each stop on the long journey.

At Kuala Lumpur station, the members of the 137 travelling on the train were reunited for a few brief moments with other 137 survivors who had been captured at Slim River and imprisoned in Kuala Lumpur. They were being transported on another train back to Singapore and incarceration in Changi, although, in the end, most of them would end up in the same camps.

En route, the train stopped on a steep gradient by a lake where everyone was able to have a swim and a wash, the first for several days.

After five days they reached Ban Pong, which is where we must leave BB and his fellow soldiers, in varying states of depression, euphoria at being alive, and apprehension as to what lay ahead, worried beyond belief about their futures, having seen the wanton cruelty dished out by the Japanese at the slightest provocation, and deeply concerned for their families. To balance things in a small way, they had each other and they were alive, but that was all.

What would the future hold? Would they see England again? When would they see Blackpool Tower on the horizon, or their loved ones waiting for them?

For some, those blessed events were denied. For BB, they came to pass in full measure giving him a rich and varied life. For him, the luck of the draw, the fortunate throw of the dice, whatever one wants to call it, certainly played a part, in addition to his personal resilience and bravery. Tennis parties and afternoon teas were long-distant memories. More than three years of hell lay ahead; but for some, sadly, much less than that.

The survivors of 137 could submit to incarceration with clear consciences. According to the eminent war historian Chye Kooi Loong, "the 11th Indian Division could indeed count itself blessed in the following field regiments for their great part of hammering the advancing Japanese units – the 155th and the 137th, the 88th and 122nd Field Regiments. The morale of the gunners never waned, and their conspicuous successes were due to the bold handling of their battery and section commanders, the efficiency and gallantry of their forward observation officers and gun teams." He continued, "in your 137 Field Regiment you lost most of the 349 and 501 Batteries at Slim River as well as your fine CO Lt. Col. Holme. Your 137 Field Regiment suffered heavy casualties and in my visits to the war cemeteries I have noted the number of the officers and men buried there: Kranji, 17; Kuala Lumpur Cheras, 31; Taiping, 17 – including your CO, Lt. Col. George Dodgson Holme."

Whilst he was in Changi, BB was able to gather his thoughts and to put them into some sort of order so that after the war, when he was asked his opinion as to whether the British units were better than the Indian, he was able to reply, "This is a difficult one. When we supported the 2nd Hydrabads, the 5/2nd Punjabs, 4/19 Hydrabads i.e. 12th Indian Infantry Brigade, we knew we would not be overrun. We did find, however, that other units tended to take fright and leave the battlefield on hearing firing behind them, a well-known Japanese subterfuge that caused problems all the way down to Singapore. The 12th Brigade were well led first by Brigadier Archibald Paris and then by Lieutenant Colonel Ian Stewart."

Brigadier Paris (born in 1890) was a serving soldier from World War 1, in which he was awarded the Military Cross in 1917.

He was given command of the 11th Indian Division until the disastrous Slim River battle, when both he and Lieutenant Ian Stewart were wounded.

After that battle, he resumed command of the 11th Indian Division for a time, but was selected by General Percival as an officer worth saving. He was ordered to leave Singapore as soon as possible, his wife having earlier escaped on the *SS Lyemoon*.

He attempted to escape on the Dutch ship *Roseboom,* which was eventually sunk by the Japanese off Sumatra. He survived the sinking, but did not survive a shocking 28-day ordeal as one of 80 passengers and crew in a single lifeboat, drifting over 100 miles with no means of navigation and from which there were only five survivors.

After Brigadier Paris had departed on his ill-fated trip, Lieutenant Ian Stewart took over, having been previously in command of the 2nd Battalion Argyll and Sutherland Highlanders. He was one of the few British officers to realise that the Japanese could only be defeated if British troops were trained to fight in jungle conditions, and he became so obsessed with this strategy that he earned himself a reputation as a crank amongst the more traditional officers. As a result of this training, the 2nd Argylls were one of the more effective units in battle.

BB was also asked his opinion of the other artillery units in the campaign. He replied, "The gunners did a grand job, but were hampered by supplies of ammo. Prior to the surrender, we requested armour-piercing shells and were told there was none in Singapore. We knew we had brought them with us on the *Perseus* (a wartime military transport) and they were, in fact, found in the Alexandra Hospital stores after the capitulation. Also, piles of dannert wire (concertina oil-tempered barbed wire) on the Straits of Johore had been in situ for years, but when we requested a supply in order to wire the site for our guns at Changi Point, before the surrender, we were unbelievably asked for appropriate documentation. We said we would take it nevertheless, but could not do so as we were told that it belonged to the Manchesters. The wire must have been in the same position in the same piles for many months or years, as the bottom three rings were under the ground. I know this to be true, because after the surrender, when we went into Changi, I supervised its removal by a Japanese working party, much to my amusement, as the other officer in the party was the one who would not let us take it in February. Our conversation was a little stilted."

BB said, "all that had happened in the Far East since we arrived in the previous November had been a complete disaster; such incompetence, a lack of awareness of the situation, and a lack of knowledge and general apathy towards the danger had made an already perilous situation many times worse".

After the war, BB was asked, "what are your feelings about the surrender?" He answered, "we had seen so much on the way down of nobody knowing what was going on and no information getting through – especially from headquarters. It seemed as though everything was done almost by word of mouth. Someone would dash along and say, 'the Japs are coming, beat it', and that's how it happened because we just didn't get any orders. What orders we got were always too late and didn't make any difference."

Whilst in Changi, the 137 could also reflect on the terrible losses sustained by the regiment. In its battle honours and on its memorials, the regiment would remember the casualties of Jitra, Slim River, Tebong, Trolak and Singapore itself, including the two men killed in the Alexandra Hospital.

In the Malayan campaign up to the surrender, the regiment lost 70 men killed or missing in action, with a further 154 destined to die in POW camps in the three years following: a total of **224** terrible losses and some 30% of the whole regiment.

This, of course, does not take into account the awful physical and mental distress of the survivors of the camps, causing suffering to all of them for the rest of their lives. Nor does it take into account several post-war suicides, one known to me, the author, personally.

Whilst BB and the other survivors of the Blackpool Regiment were fighting prior to the surrender on 15th February, a flotilla of ships was desperately trying to escape, most of them destined to be destroyed before reaching their destinations.

My uncle Ronnie would be one of the many casualties.

PART TWO

THE SINKING OF HMS YIN PING

7. SINGAPORE 1942

Tugboat *HMS Yin Ping* (105 feet long, 191 gross tons)

I am now going to tell the story of the sinking of *HMS Yin Ping*, and the death of my uncle Ronnie, who died with many others in the most tragic of circumstances. I will also tell the stories of a few of the survivors of the sinking, some lucky to be alive, others not so, and those who ultimately perished.

It is my intention to pay tribute to all the brave men and one woman who sailed on *HMS Yin Ping* and, by extension, to pay tribute to everyone caught up in the surrender and partial naval evacuation of the hell that was Singapore.

****

Francis Ronald Emery 1913-1942

You will no doubt recall that we left BB and his fellow soldiers and officers in Ban Pong, having been moved from Changi POW camp.

There they must stay for the moment as we transport ourselves back in time and place to the centre of Singapore, and to the few days prior to the surrender.

On 10th February 1942, the last few RAF aircraft left Singapore, ceding control of the skies to the Japanese, and abandoning all ground crew, including Ronnie, leaving them to make their way to the port as best they could. The situation in the port, as well as in the city itself, was desperate.

On 11th February, the capture of the high ground around Bukit Timah Hill enabled the Japanese to refine the bombardment of Singapore, increasing it in ferocity and improving in accuracy.

On 12th February, the three city reservoirs had been captured.

To prevent any remaining ships falling into enemy hands, the senior naval officer, Rear Admiral Ernest Spooner, decreed that all ships should sail by Friday 13th February, and head for Java or Sumatra.

Rear Admiral Ernest Spooner DSO (born 1887) took up his post in Malaya in 1941. At the time of the Japanese invasion later that year, he had two superior Admirals, Sir Tom Phillips and Vice Admiral Jeffrey Layton, but sadly Admiral Phillips was killed when his flagship *Prince of Wales* was sunk on 10th December 1941.

To make matters worse, on 5th January 1942 Vice Admiral Layton moved his headquarters to the island of Java, leaving Ernest Spooner as senior naval officer in Malaya.

By 12th February, most naval personnel including Ernest Spooner's wife, the noted soprano Megan Foster, had left on the merchantman *Empire Star*. But Ernest Spooner and a few others remained behind to assist in the evacuation of civilians.

From the story of *HMS Yin Ping* it will become clear that the whole evacuation was a dismal, diabolical affair, many ships being destroyed by the Japanese naval and air forces as they left the port.

One of the many vessels caught up in the attempted escape was HMML (Motor Launch) *310* transporting Rear Admiral Spooner, Air Vice Marshal Conway Pulford and some 40 others. The vessel was attacked by Japanese aircraft, but managed to limp to Chibia, a small uninhabited island some 200 miles from Singapore. Despite the lack of fresh water, the stranded survivors lasted two months before disease and starvation forced them to surrender. By that time, both Spooner and Pulford had died of exhaustion and malaria. Safely back in England, Megan Spooner eventually heard of the loss of her husband. In due course, she managed to resume her singing career, performing regularly on the BBC Home Service. She died in 1987, never having really recovered from her husband's death.

Singapore was in chaos. Imagine the scene. The incessant shelling and bombing had taken their toll. Plumes of charcoal smoke arose from the rubble-strewn streets. Dirt. Debris. Destruction everywhere. Wreckage from buildings blocked pavements and damaged roads. Bombs pounded the green spaces from Singapore's past calm and happy existence. What was once a colourful and vibrant city was now washed out in shades of dirty grey. In the far distance, the silhouette of a bus could be seen, its sides caved in, with jagged mangled metal jutting out at odd angles. An enormous crane, minutes previously standing tall, now lay collapsed, creating a barrier denying entry to all.

A row of parked cars had been scattered, each coming to rest at random. Some lay on their sides, some on their roofs. All obliterated. Their outlines were barely recognisable, save for the shredded tyres and the smoking rubber further polluting the choking air.

Shells of buildings overlooked the carnage on the road, skeletons with broken bricks and charred timbers emerged from the drifting smoke which obliterated them from view for minutes at a time and then, ghost-like, they would reappear. Far beyond the buildings, shells could be seen exploding on the water, sending up cascading plumes of red and orange.

There were many bodies in the debris. They would never have dreamt that their final resting place would be in the midst of a war zone. Over the noise could be heard the mournful barking of dogs being taken by their owners to be humanely put down.

On 12 February 1942, Ronnie with several remaining RAF ground staff were transported through the burning city to the chaos of the port. They offloaded in a state of bewilderment and fear and were hustled on to *HMS Trang*. Captained by Lieutenant H.G. Rigden, this was a converted whaler and formerly used as a patrol vessel, but was now assisting in the evacuation of Singapore, transporting some 50 RAF personnel, 21 other service personnel and 10 crew.

Also in the port at anchor was *HMS Yin Ping*, the ship that was to carry the destinies of so many people.

HMS Yin Ping, 105 foot long, weighing 191 gross tons, was a tugboat originally designed to assist in the berthing of ships and the towing of barges in mainland China and Hong Kong. Built in 1914, it was owned by the Chinese Dredger Company which had been formed in China in 1917 to cooperate in shipping matters with the Kailan Mining Administration. The Administration had significant mining assets, particularly coal mines in Tientsin, in northern China. However, the Administration's assets were subject to attacks by Japanese rebels in 1924, and so *HMS Yin Ping* was sent to safety in Singapore, where it continued with its tugboat duties until, in 1941, it was requisitioned by the Royal Navy.

8. RONALD EMERY

Ronnie's father and my maternal grandfather, James Frederick Emery, was born on 17th December 1886 in Shevington, a coal mining village near Wigan in Lancashire.

James' father, and Ronnie's grandfather, William Emery originally came from Chew Magna, a small village in Somerset, where he was described as a labourer in the 1881 census.

Later that year, or early in the following year, he decided that there was no future for him in the Somerset backwater, so he decided to walk to Wigan to find work in the pits. It is some 185 miles from Chew Magna to Wigan. Walking at a steady pace for a few hours each day and resting at night, the journey would have probably taken about nine or 10 days.

In those days, Wigan was a major coal mining area. At the time of William's journey, there were nearly a thousand pits (mostly open cast) in the Wigan area alone, the first pit having been opened in 1450, only 35 years after the Battle of Agincourt.

On arriving in Wigan, he not only found work in the pits, but also found a wife as well, first living with Ruth Dootson, and then marrying her. From her photograph, Ruth looks to be a formidable lady, but in fairness the photograph was almost certainly taken later in life.

They lived in Lower Ground, Standish, in a one-up, one-down cottage. Needless to say, even though William had a good job by the standards of the time, the family were very poor. Indeed, at that time most of the country was poor.

In his later years, my grandfather would often tell the story of how a goat had wandered into the village one night. In those days there was no animal protection or sentiment so the goat was dispatched forthwith, and roasted on an open fire for the benefit of all.
William worked hard in the pits, and he was eventually appointed to be a check weighman. This meant that he had to agree the weight of coal mined in each shift with the check weighman acting for the owners, as miners were then paid by the weight of coal actually mined.

William and Ruth Emery produced five children: Winifred, William, Mary Ann, Harry and Ronnie's father, my maternal grandfather, James Frederick, whose life we will briefly follow. In those days it was usual for sons to follow their fathers into the pits. Young James Frederick, however, was different. He was educated at the local Crook School, where the headmaster, Mr James Lyon, spotted potential in young Fred, so that when he eventually left school in 1899, aged 13, Fred's parents were persuaded to let him join the Lancashire and Yorkshire Railway. This he did, becoming a telegraphist at Gathurst Station, Wigan, in December 1899.

His working week was 72 hours, 6am to 5pm Monday to Saturday and 9am to 3pm Sunday, followed by an easy week of 56 hours. He still somehow found time to study, teaching himself shorthand and typing, using a cardboard imitation of a typewriter keyboard which he bought for a few pence.

In 1906 he was placed in the district manager's office in Bolton, where his ever-increasing thirst for knowledge led him to evening classes and examination success. The directors of the railway company awarded him a scholarship to Manchester University, where he studied economics under Professor Sidney Chapman. His education was to serve him well in later life. Apparently, he passed his exams but was unable to afford the few shillings which were required to confirm his degree, and he was never able to call himself a B. Econ.

He married Florence Beatrice Gradwell on 15th of April 1912. This was the day the Titanic sank, and grandfather used to comment jokingly, in later life, that there were two disasters on the same day.

In July 1914, he was appointed to be the general manager of a group of Indian Light Railways, but his intended emigration to India was interrupted by the outbreak of war. He enlisted in the Lancashire Fusiliers, but was immediately transferred back to the railways as his occupation, like farmers and miners, was deemed to be protected. Almost certainly, his work saved his life because the Lancashire Fusiliers were sent to Gallipoli, where the casualties were horrific.

In 1916 or 1917, while still working on the railway, he talked his brother Billy into hiring the local village hall and a cinema projector. They hung up a sheet for a screen, one of them took the money on the door, and the other turned the handle on the projector. Thus, my grandfather's cinema empire began.

However, notwithstanding the success of the venture, brother Billy decided that the cinema business was not for him after all. He became a bus driver, although the two brothers always remained close.

Grandfather's other brother, Harry, fought through the First World War, survived, bemedaled, but unscathed physically. After the war he went back to work as a clerk on the railways.

Sister Winifred married a butcher and went to live in Anglesey, while sister Mary Ann married Frederick Gore and lived in Altrincham.

My grandfather continued to run his cinema business, taking properties on short-term leases as he had no capital to invest in the buildings. He also became politically minded, and in 1921 was elected to be a local Tory Councillor in Salford, thus starting his political career more or less at the same time as his business empire.

Of course, this story is not really about my grandfather.

However, his story has been briefly told as it sets out the kind of life that Ronnie would have come home to and would have enjoyed, had he survived the sinking of *HMS Yin Ping*, and the almost certain incarceration thereafter.

Grandfather's cinema business flourished at a time when there was nothing to compete with it. Television was in the future. Theatres and music hall were old hat. Cinemas were new and exciting.

One of his Manchester cinemas employed a full orchestra to play accompanying music and to fill in at the intervals. Then along came talking pictures further swelling admissions. From the days of the early talkies in the late 1920s to the late 1940s he acquired nearly 100 cinemas in places as diverse as Bradford, Blackpool, Bristol, Cardiff, Derby, Huddersfield, Westbury and Wimbledon.

Remember the magic of the cinema experience? The usherettes with their all-seeing torches and their ice cream trays, the doormen with their braided uniforms, the trailers for next week's offering, the interval music, the still photographs outside the cinema, and the waves of laughter or tears dependent on what was portrayed on the screen...such magic indeed.

Parallel with the cinema business, grandfather was pursuing a political career. He was a firm believer in private enterprise and fair competition, but he was also conscious of the unfairness of the rule of the privileged classes and the injustice of the class system.

He became leader of Salford council in 1931, and in 1935 became Mayor.

In the same year, he was elected Conservative MP for Salford West and served for 10 years under three Prime Ministers...Baldwin, Chamberlain and Churchill....10 years of the most exciting and momentous events in British history, including the Abdication and World War II.

Pre-war, he was a member of various Parliamentary delegations visiting Egypt, France, Belgium and Germany, where prior to Munich he met Hitler, Göring and Goebbels, and others of that infamous gang.

He stood a few feet away from Hitler at the 1937 Nuremberg rally, having gone to Germany to see what could be learned about the construction of German autobahns.

His proudest achievement was to sit on the committee which formulated the basis of the NHS. Unfortunately, he did not survive the Labour landslide of the 1945 election, so he was unable to participate in the actual establishment of the NHS in 1947.

In 1942, he purchased Illawalla, an extraordinary building on the Fylde Coast, reputedly the biggest bungalow in Europe complete with 10 bedrooms, five bathrooms, billiard room, ballroom, a tower, a minaret and a green copper dome, together with 15 acres of gardens, parks and pastures. It was occupied by the army at the time, but then became a convalescent home for pregnant refugees.

Needless to say it was in substantial need of repair.

When you think about it, it was an astonishing statement of confidence, as in 1942 it was by no means certain that Britain would emerge victorious from the war.

So Ronnie, had he lived , would have been coming back to an immensely profitable business, to a much-respected family, a father politically involved and well known and liked, having just purchased the most magnificent house.

As we know, it was not to be. He would never see his father knighted (as he was in 1960), nor would he see him live to the venerable old age of 96. He would be spared the tragedies which afflicted his brother Gordon, with the loss of his wife Joan, and later the death of his son Bobby in a car accident, followed by his own early death at 65 from prostate cancer. He would also have been spared the tragic death of his sister, my mother.
As we know life throws these tragedies at everyone on an almost

daily basis, and my grandfather certainly had his share....wealth, success and tragedies in equal measure.

Francis Ronald Emery (Ronnie) was born on 31st January 1913 whilst my grandfather and his wife Florence were living at 82 Gathurst Lane, Shevington. Grandfather was still on the railways, but with his brother Billy was dreaming of better things, the cinema idea hatching in their minds.

In due course, grandfather's employment on the railways enabled him and his wife Florence to move from Shevington, Wigan, and their small cottage, to Bolton Road, Salford, some 30 miles or so away. Salford was to become grandfather's home for the next 30 years.

Ronnie attended Halton Bank Council School before going to Manchester Grammar School in 1925 as a foundation scholar, although he did not distinguish himself academically. He left school in 1929, and my grandfather decided that Ronnie should have a profession. He arranged for him to be articled to a firm of accountants in Manchester, where he studied for three years, only to fail his exams at the end of his training period. It was clear that accountancy was not for him, so grandfather took him into his cinema business, which had been expanding during the time of Ronnie's education and training. By the time war came along in 1939, Ronnie was a director of a large and thriving business, being responsible for booking the films to be shown at the various cinemas. It was envisaged that he would take over the whole business from his father one day.

In addition, Ronnie had always had a passion for flying, so he joined the Royal Air Force Volunteer Reserve in 1938, aged 25.

The RAFVR was formed in 1936 to provide additional help to the Auxiliary Air Force, which had been formed in 1925 by various local TA associations. The Auxiliary Air Force was organised into squadrons, with local recruitment similar to the Territorial Army, so initially all the members of the RAFVR were civilians, recruited from local neighbourhoods. Recruits had to be between 18 and 25, and accepted as part time training as pilots, observers or wireless operators. The object was to provide a reserve of aircrew in the event of war. In this task it succeeded, so that in 1939 there were 6,646 pilots, 1,625 observers, and 1,946 wireless operators in reserve, all ready and willing to serve.

**RAF Evanton personnel with Ronnie Emery
(front row, fourth from right)**

On the outbreak of war, Ronnie volunteered and was sent to RAF Padgate, a training camp in the Fearnhead district of Warrington, Cheshire. This small RAF station was formed in April 1939 as an air-crew holding unit. It became a receiving centre in May 1939 and a recruiting centre in January 1940. This would have been Ronnie's first taste of military discipline, with ill-fitting uniforms and a severe haircut. The buildings were of wooden construction. Huts were set out in neat rows, with nearby ablutions. In each hut was a round heating stove. The floors (and everything else) were highly polished and spick and span. There was more than one cookhouse and dining hall and several squares for drilling. The staff were all male, including those in the NAAFI. Ronnie would have been allocated a hut and issued with a knife, fork and spoon and a large white china mug. By all accounts, the food was 'excellent'.

Daily drill and inspections were performed on the parade squares under the 'drill pigs', mostly acting corporal drill instructors, although a senior NCO sometimes supervised. Fatigue parties at the training camps were also normal and these might have included collecting swill from the messes and feeding it to the camp pigs. Other fatigues also included street cleaning and painting kerbs white and keeping grass neat.

RAF Padgate comprised men from every corner of the British Isles, the majority training as flight mechanics and flight riggers (although there were also plenty of other trades). Foot drill and arms drill were initially carried out in civilian clothes until uniform was issued and tailored to fit. The men were instructed on how to make beds, leaving them neat and tidy, with blankets and sheets neatly folded. All huts had to be kept meticulously clean.

All RAFVR ground trades were informed by post/telegram that they would be called up when 'space' became available. Until then, they were deferred and could continue with their 'civilian' occupation.

Following completion of his training, Ronnie was posted to RAF Evanton in Scotland as an RAF military policeman, with an acting rank of corporal. In a letter to his brother Gordon, he gave details of the arduous journey from Padgate to Evanton, leaving at 3:30 pm one Friday and, after constantly changing trains, arriving at 9:30 pm the next day (Saturday). The train was overcrowded, and he was forced to stand in full kit for 300 of the 400-mile journey.

In the same letter he describes Evanton as, "the edge of beyond" and "in the wilds". He noted that the nearest cinema was eight miles away and that there was no show in the camp. He also went on to lament the lack of transport. He complained that unless you had a car to get to Inverness to the pictures (about 12 miles away) there was absolutely nothing to do at night except sit in the NAAFI boozing. He joked with his brother, "if anytime you feel you don't need 'Ken' (Gordon's car) just ship it up here!" Indeed, such a boring routine often forced Ronnie to retire to bed at 7:30pm when he was not on duty.

Despite its remote geographical location, when RAF Evanton was open to the public on Empire Day 1939 it attracted a mile-long queue of cars and 9,000 visitors. It appeared that discipline was not particularly severe and that there was very little cleaning of huts. A typical overnight shift was from midnight to 8 am. After that, all the next day until the following morning at 7:30 am would be free.

So how did Ronnie end up in the Port of Singapore on the night of the 12th February about to board *HMS Trang*?

It is almost certain that he, along with other RAF personnel, was transported to Malaya via troopship. Air travel was not an option, unless the serviceman being transported was of high enough rank or importance to warrant travel by air.

All the known facts about Ronnie suggest that he was transported to Malaya in the same convoy as BB, perhaps even on the same ship, the Dominion Monarch, and it is interesting to speculate that BB and Ronnie might have shared a drink, as they were both originally from the Manchester area.

Some collaborative evidence for this journey comes from the official diary for 512 Air Ministry Experimental Station, a radar station at Bukit Tanjong Kupang, which stated that the arrival of four service police were expected on the 5th December 1941. There is no actual proof that Ronnie was one of these, but the date of the expected arrival is given shortly after the *Dominion Monarch* anchored in Singapore.

Perhaps more than just a coincidence? In any event, on arrival in Malaya Ronnie was first posted to RAF Kallang, where he was on a standby filter flight, a personnel holding flight from which one could be attached straight away to any station or unit within Malaya, whenever and wherever extra manpower was needed. Until that point, he would be carrying out his duties at Kallang.

Kallang airport was the first purpose-built civil international airport in Singapore, officially opened on 12th June 1937. As well as the usual ground landing facilities, the airport boasted an anchorage area for seaplanes, and was hailed as, "the finest airport in the British Empire".

Ronnie, now in Malaya, shortly to be in Singapore, was inexorably moving towards his fate.

9. HMS YIN PING SAILS

Singapore was a chaotic mess.

Early in February, all ocean-going vessels still remaining in the port were commandeered by the authorities to assist in the evacuation of as many people as possible.

Up to then, civilians were only allowed to leave with a departure pass issued by the colonial government authorities. Men under 40 were barred from leaving the island altogether, and women were not publicly encouraged to leave because of the adverse effect on morale.

However, on about 11th January 1942 the difficulties of the situation became increasingly clear and departure passes were issued more or less at random.

The evacuation fleet, comprised ships of varying sizes, from the cargo ship *SS Empire Star* (525 feet long and weighing 12,656 tonnes) down to the smallest coastal craft like the *SS Tanjong Pinang* which at 97 feet in length, only just qualified as a 'ship.' There was some confusion about the number of ships in the fleet. Estimates vary between 55 and 60. All in all, there were at least 5,000 intended evacuees and about 900 personnel manning the various craft.

Other ships, although not part of the official evacuation fleet, attempted to escape as well.

In truth, more or less any ocean going vessel of any size was commandeered by the authorities to assist with the evacuation.

This fleet was assembled to leave in convoy between 11th and 13th February.

In addition to the fleet of commandeered ships there were several naval ships, including a couple of destroyers, which briefly escorted the larger merchant ships like the *SS Empire Star* and the *SS Gorgon*.

'Naval ships' included any ship which had been requisitioned by the navy, as opposed to being commandeered by the civilian authorities. The naval ships carried service personnel only, although as in the case of *HMS Yin Ping* a few civilians were allowed on board.

Of the ships leaving Singapore, only six would eventually make it to safety.

The fates of the other ships varied. Some were sunk, some ran aground. Many were captured at sea by the Japanese navy, their passengers and crews either killed there and then, or taken prisoner to face three-and-a-half years of harsh treatment in internment or in POW camps.

On the afternoon of Friday 13th February 1942, *HMS Yin Ping* was anchored off Clifford Pier, Singapore Harbour. It was commanded by Lieutenant Patrick Wilkinson acting under the overall orders of Captain Atkinson.

The number of those on board has never been exactly calculated, because the original crew numbers were never accurately stated.

Captain Atkinson put the total number at 78 (crew and passengers), other reports at slightly less than that.

At some time in the afternoon of 13th February, Captain Atkinson and Lieutenant Wilkinson boarded.

Later, at 17:00 hours, *HMS Yin Ping* was also boarded by Commander Douglas, Captain R.P. Chapman, Mr Leigh Hunt,

Yeoman of Signals Mockford, Petty Officer Ritchie, five seaman ratings, two royal marines and Alice Wilkinson, Lieutenant Wilkinson's wife, who had been given special permission to board by Captain Atkinson.

Captain Kenneth Atkinson was Admiral Spooner's Chief of Staff, and in effect the Captain of the Dockyard. He was to leave Singapore Harbour on *HMS Yin Ping* about the same time as Rear Admiral Spooner and Air Vice Marshall Conway Pulford were leaving on the ill-fated Motor Launch *310*.

Captain Thomas Kenneth Whitmore Atkinson was born in 1902, in Wakefield Yorkshire, the son of Corkett Wadsley Atkinson and Constance Mary Atkinson. He attended Royal Naval colleges at Osborne and Dartmouth between the years 1915-1918 and was appointed midshipman in 1919. During the post-war years he spent time on a series of warships including *HMS Warspite*, *HMS Versatile* and the battlecruiser *HMS Repulse*. By 1923, he had been appointed lieutenant and then joined *HMS Hood* for two years. He attended navigation courses between 1926 and 1935, and was promoted to lieutenant commander in 1931 before being promoted further to navigation officer on ships operating from Devonport and Portsmouth. By 1934 he was made a full commander.

His meteoric rise did not stop there. In 1938 following more staff courses, he was made a navigating officer aboard the cruiser *HMS London*. Between 1938 and 1940 he was executive officer (commander) of *HMS Nelson,* then being promoted to the rank of captain. Shortly afterwards, he was appointed Captain of Dockyard, Deputy Superintendent and King's Harbourmaster of H.M. Dockyard, Singapore. It was here, on the afternoon of Friday 13th February 1942, that he joined *HMS Yin Ping* on her last voyage, having stayed too long in Singapore before eventually receiving orders from Rear Admiral Spooner to proceed to Batavia, then the capital of the Dutch East Indies, and now the modern city of Jakarta, the capital of Indonesia.

HMS Yin Ping was actually commanded by Lieutenant Wilkinson RNR, even though he was of lower rank than Captain Atkinson.

Lieutenant Patrick Howard Wilkinson was born on 11th February 1912 (by coincidence the same year as BB), in Melbourne, Australia.

He was educated at Melbourne Church of England Grammar School and started his working life as a tea planter in Ceylon. He then became an assistant planter on the Baradin Rubber Estate, Paloh, Johore.

In July 1940, he enlisted in the Straits Settlement Royal Naval Volunteer Reserve, being appointed acting sub-lieutenant later in that year. He also married Alice Gwendolyne Bradgate at St. Andrew's Cathedral, Singapore, holding their wedding reception on board the ship he was commanding at the time. By special permission, as fate would have it, Alice was able to join her husband on *HMS Yin Ping*.

Commander Berwick Maitland Douglas (born 1900) attended the merchant navy training school as a young boy on *HMS Conway*, moored in Merseyside, a 19th century wooden 'ship of the line'. He was commissioned in 1918 as a sub-lieutenant in the Royal Navy, then became a lieutenant in 1921. It is possible that he returned to the merchant navy world during peacetime but in 1939 he volunteered and was appointed an acting lieutenant in the Royal Navy. Three years later he is described as 'Lieutenant Commander R.N. (retired)'. At the start of the war in the Far East, in 1941, he appeared in Singapore as a 'Passive Defence Officer, H.M. Naval Base' and for a year or so was delivering talks across the Malayan Broadcasting Service on topics such as, 'The Naval Situation', where his purpose was to amplify the rather bare Admiralty statements concerning British naval activities.

He appeared in a photograph taken in 1940, attending the 'Conway-Worcester' Old Boys Association dinner at the Adelphi, Singapore, dining alongside another fellow *HMS Conway* old boy – Lt. Basil Shaw, who would also lose his life whilst escaping Singapore.

Hereford-born Engineer Captain Roland Paul Chapman had entered the Royal Navy in 1912 at the tender age of 15. Two years later he was appointed a midshipman on *HMS Hannibal*. His WW1 service included *HMS Benbow*, *HMS Mignonette*, and the destroyer *HMS Christopher*. After WW1, he was appointed a lieutenant and served on the torpedo boat destroyer *HMS Valentine* before entering engineering colleges at Greenwich and Plymouth. By 1921, he had joined the battleship *HMS Warspite*. Three years later he moved to the cruiser *HMS Calcutta*, gaining promotion to lieutenant commander. In 1926 he returned to working in the engineering department at HM Dockyard at Chatham. He was then appointed commander on the battleship *HMS Rodney* in 1929, and in the following year he was back at the engineering department before joining the cruiser *HMS Diomede*, in 1933. Further promotion was gained in 1936 to engineering inspector, Engineer in Chief's Department, Admiralty, during which time he was made engineer captain. Five years later, he travelled out to Singapore in the role of engineer captain, arriving about the same time the Japanese invaded northern Malaya.

John Leigh Hunt was one of the few civilians on *HMS Yin Ping*. He was employed in the Works Department in Singapore but very little is known about him. References were made about him in pre-war Singapore newspapers acknowledging him as a polo player. He is recorded as riding Sweet Diana in the Singapore gymkhana of 1941, a rare glimpse of normality in a world shortly to destroy itself.

James Winsor Mockford (known as Mogger) was born in 1900 in Kincardine, Scotland. He had served on *HMS Repulse* as a yeoman of signals.

Petty Officer Leonard David Ritchie, aged 33, was a member of Captain Atkinson's staff, born in Kent to parents David and Louisa Ritchie.

Shortly after boarding, Captain Atkinson returned to shore to assist with the embarkation of troops who were being evacuated from *HMS Grasshopper* and *HMS Scorpion*.

He came back on board just before midnight. Shortly after that shells began to fall around *HMS Yin Ping* and she was ordered to weigh anchor and leave the port, which she did at 23:50 hours on

13th February, with a motor launch, the *Eureka*, manned by Petty Officer McFarling and Mechanic Sillcock, in tow.

It was a very dark night, visibility being further diminished by the smoke from the various fuel depots deliberately set on fire in order to avoid their contents falling into enemy hands.

At 00:15 on Saturday 14th February, *HMS Yin Ping* passed Coopers Channel and approached Peak Island (also known as Kusu Island, three-and-a-half miles south of Singapore), where it was apparent that *HMS Trang*, with Commander Alexander in charge, was in trouble and had run ashore.

HMS Yin Ping released the *Eureka* with Commander Douglas in charge to assist *HMS Trang* from which he managed to transfer *to HMS Yin Ping* between 50 and 70 army and air force other ranks, including Ronnie.

Eventually *HMS Trang* was re-floated, but to avoid it falling into enemy hands it was set on fire in Cooper's Channel and abandoned. Twenty-six persons (personnel and crew) who could not be transferred from *HMS Trang* made it back to shore but were captured and became POWS.

Nearby the *SS Hong Tat* went aground, but no further assistance could be rendered due to the lack of space on *HMS Yin Ping*, which was carrying a large quantity of coal on her deck and could not accommodate any more passengers with safety. Overloaded and having re-attached the launch *Eureka*, at 02:20 *HMS Yin Ping* continued its journey westward.

At this time, the smoke was particularly bad, with visibility almost down to zero and so at 03:30 it was decided to anchor.

At 04:00 on 14 February, *HMS Yin Ping* spotted Fairmile Motor Launch *310*, with Admiral Spooner on board. It was having difficulty with its steering gear and had run aground. *HMS Yin Ping* offered assistance, but it was declined, and the ML eventually proceeded ahead of *HMS Yin Ping* notwithstanding its problems, en-route to its fate in Chibia.

At 06:50 after a problem with a shearing pin, *HMS Yin Ping* entered the Darian Strait. Despite being extremely visible, *HMS Yin Ping* remained unmolested by the Japanese aircraft flying continually overhead.

Later in the morning, on 14th February, *HMS Yin Ping* came across the water boat *Daisy,* which appeared to be lost and was struggling to make way. Unfortunately, the *Daisy* had no charts and *HMS Yin Ping* agreed to meet her at False Durian Island.

About 12:45 on the 14th, *HMS Yin Ping* sighted *HMS Malacca*, anchored close in shore near False Durian Island, contact having been re-established with the *Daisy*.

HMS Malacca, 210 tonnes, launched in 1927, served as a minesweeper between 1939 and 1942. Requisitioned, she was assisting with the evacuation. She eventually made it to Sumatra, and after delivering her evacuees, she was scuttled on 18th February on the Tjemako River.

HMS Yin Ping and *Daisy* closed in on the *Malacca* with the intention of remaining with it until dark in order to avoid the enemy aircraft which were attacking all vessels attempting to escape. The captain of the *Malacca* was not at all happy that his ship was being used to protect *HMS Yin Ping* and the *Daisy*.

However, whilst they were anchored, 20 army other ranks were transferred from *HMS Yin Ping* to the *Daisy,* thus easing *Yin Ping*'s load.

At 13:10 hours on the 14th, enemy aircraft attacked the ships, *HMS Yin Ping* being the subject of a very near hit. This caused panic on the overcrowded tugboat. In the chaos, the *Eureka* launch, which was then still attached to *HMS Yin Ping,* somehow detached itself, ran on to a reef and sank.

HMS Yin Ping quickly cast off from the Malacca and anchored further away in two fathoms, where it was discovered that the exploding bombs had filled the port side with water, causing a heavy list.

The *Daisy* then ran ashore and had to be towed off.

To ease *HMS Yin Ping*'s load still further, the army personnel on board were transferred to the *Malacca*, but then the *Malacca*'s condenser cracked, so *HMS Yin Ping* had to stand by until

The Final Journey of *HMS Yin Ping*

Location of Singapore

it was repaired.

Of course, all these relatively small matters conspired to eventually place *HMS Yin Ping* at the time and place where she would meet her fate.

Eventually, *HMS Yin Ping*, the *Malacca* and the *Daisy* decided to risk all and go ahead. However, during the night of the 14th/15th February, *HMS Yin Ping* lost contact with both ships and proceeded alone, setting a course for the Bangka Strait to arrive at sunset on Sunday 15th February, by which time they would be some 300 miles from Singapore.

Alas, it was not to be.

On the 15th, *HMS Yin Ping* was making good progress. Berhala Island (already occupied by the Japanese, and later to become a temporary internment camp) was passed at 10:00. Eventually at 17:45, Bangka Island, some 334 miles from Singapore, was sighted. Unfortunately, and unknown to those at sea, the island had also been captured by the Japanese in early February, and so was no longer a safe haven for any escapees.

Captain Atkinson was on watch at this time, but at 19:20 Lieutenant Wilkinson came back to the bridge, to discover that there were two Japanese ships on the port quarter about two miles away, a cruiser and a destroyer.

The cruiser signalled to *HMS Yin Ping* and then trained a searchlight on her.

Lieutenant Wilkinson gave orders for all personnel to get out of sight, but at 19:25 the cruiser opened fire from a range of about 3,000 yards.

The first salvo hit the bridge, where it appeared that everyone was killed or seriously wounded apart from Lieutenant Wilkinson, his wife and Captain Atkinson, who were nevertheless all badly cut by shell splinters. To make matters worse, fire immediately broke out so that the three of them were forced to leave the bridge as quickly as they could.

An unnamed survivor who was on the bridge with Captain Atkinson remembered him saying, as they watched the cruiser, "this may be our last moment". Immediately after that he said, "they have fired".

Casualties of the first attack included Mr Leigh Hunt, who was blown overboard from the bridge as the first shell struck, and Yeoman of Signals Mockford, who was standing where the first salvo struck and was never seen again.

The second salvo hit the foredeck causing many casualties, and the third damaged the boiler, killing a large number of men near the engine room.

The gun fire from the Japanese ships was intense. *HMS Yin Ping*'s decks were littered with dead and wounded, and she was burning furiously. Nevertheless, she was still managing to make some small headway. However, at 19:30 further progress became impossible, so the chief engineer ordered the engine room to be evacuated and the main engine shut down.

By now, *HMS Yin Ping* was listing badly, and it was impossible to remain on the foredeck. The midway section was also on fire so the order was given to abandon ship.

Amidst the terrible chaos Lieutenant Wilkinson saw that Commander Douglas had been badly wounded with two broken arms, two broken legs and was in terrible pain. It is assumed that he died shortly thereafter, as clearly he could not have survived the sinking and the struggle to board the one serviceable lifeboat.

According to Admiralty records, Commander Douglas was "missing, presumed dead". On a sad note, it is not known whether Commander Douglas was married or had children. He perished as though he had never been, and his manner of death, whether by shellfire or drowning, remains unknown.

About 19:45 *HMS Yin Ping* was listing further to starboard and was clearly sinking, which it did in less than a minute. As it was sinking all hands were ordered to jump clear. There were two lifeboats, starboard and port. The starboard boat was in flames and too badly damaged to be usable. A large quantity of .303 ammunition was stored near the port boat, and was intermittently exploding. However, Lieutenant Wilkinson, with the help of several naval ratings, succeeded in launching this boat, righting it even when it capsized, and finally loading it with personnel.

Efforts were made to keep the one lifeboat clear of the sinking ship. Lieutenant Wilkinson ordered that the wounded should be kept on the boat, and those free of wounds should remain in the water, clinging where possible to lines attached to the lifeboat. Unfortunately, one oar was missing from the lifeboat, and it was impossible to row to and reach those people who had left *HMS Yin Ping* by the foredeck.

The Japanese cruiser responsible for sinking *HMS Yin Ping* came back to have a look at the damage, but offered no assistance.

The survivors in the lifeboat and those attached to it were only a few miles from the coast of Bangka Island near the Muntok lighthouse, but virtually no progress was being made as the tide turned against them.

About midday on 16th February two RAF launches were spotted. They came to the assistance of Lieutenant Wilkinson and the other survivors and took them to Muntok Pier, where all survivors, probably about 20 in all, were taken as prisoners of war by the Japanese, who had captured Bangka Island some days earlier and who had set up a temporary POW camp at Muntok. The Japanese closed this camp in mid-March 1942 but reopened it later for a period of 18 months from September 1943.

Others from *HMS Yin Ping* survived the sinking. Some swam or paddled to Bangka Island where they were summarily executed by the Japanese patrols.

Some made it into the jungle on Bangka Island where they held out for a few days. Others hid in the village of Rambat on the north coast of the Island for up to three weeks before they were eventually captured.

Those that survived instant execution on capture, were held at Muntok before being shipped to Palembang POW camp, Sumatra. They were transported by small boats across the Bangka Strait. On arrival in Sumatra, they were transported up the Musi River to Palembang Camp, a mixed civilian and military internment camp.

Civilian men and women were separated and held in the jail and various residences in the town.

The military were separated into three camps: the Mulo School, the Chung Wa School and Sungei Geron.

The journey up the Musi took 12 hours and was very uncomfortable. The prisoners' only subsistence was a handful of cold rice and some sips of tepid water. There was no protection from the sun, and the only toilet facility was a wooden plank projecting above the water upon which one had to balance precariously.

Many regretted having survived the sinking.

It turned out that *HMS Yin Ping* had the misfortune to meet the light cruisers *Yura* and *Sendai,* and the destroyers *Asagri* and *Fubuki*, which were providing protection for the Japanese invasion fleet heading for Sumatra.

The *Sendai* was the ship that sent *HMS Yin Ping* to the bottom of the Bangka Strait. It was a large ship, 418 feet in length, 5,200 tons, and carried seven turrets of 5.5-inch guns.

What a tragic mismatch!

10. THE SINKING – THE AFTERMATH

HMS Yin Ping was history. Who perished? Who survived?

Of the estimated 78 people on board (including 50 RAF men), it is thought that there were 32 survivors. However, it is only known what happened to a small proportion of them.

You will no doubt recall that there were several people who boarded the ship at 17:00 hours on 13th February 1942, two days and a lifetime before the sinking. We know that Leigh Hunt and Yeoman Mockford were killed when the first salvo hit. Killed along with them were Petty Officer Ritchie, 33 years old, from Rainham in Kent, husband of Helena Elsie Ritchie, a member of Captain Atkinson's staff, together with another civilian, John Thompson Bonar. He had been sent to Malaya in 1924 as an assistant conservator of forests. In 1940 he had been promoted to senior assistant conservator of forests, but he had stayed behind in Singapore having said goodbye to his wife Mary and their three daughters, who had left on the *Nashula* and had successfully made it to Victoria, Australia.

We also know that Commander Douglas was terribly wounded and is assumed to have died when *HMS Yin Ping* sank, as did the badly wounded Captain Atkinson, who left behind his wife Mary and three children. He was 42.

Mrs Wilkinson also drowned when the ship sank.

Lieutenant Wilkinson survived the sinking and became a prisoner of war, somehow surviving his captivity.

Captain Chapman was captured and made a POW in Muntok before moving to Palembang. He also survived his captivity and was eventually appointed Captain and Commanding Officer of the Royal Navy Training Establishment in Cornwall before spending two years as ADC to George VI. He eventually died in 1959 in Radnorshire.

The workings of fate are strange. My grandfather was eventually told of Ronnie's death, although exactly when he was informed is not known. He certainly knew nothing of the exact circumstances of his son's death. He had merely been "killed in action, in the fall of Singapore".

Some time after the war, my grandfather was visited by John Stanley Livingstone. Like Ronnie, he had been a corporal in the RAF and had been on *HMS Yin Ping* with him. Corporal Livingstone (in the passenger list referred to as John Stanley Swingstone) had been praised by Lieutenant Wilkinson for assisting in the launching of the only seaworthy lifeboat and being directly responsible for the righting of it after it had capsized. He survived the sinking, and was captured on 16th February 1942. He became a prisoner of war in Muntok and Palembang.

He told my grandfather he had been with Ronnie when *HMS Yin Ping* was struck and eventually sank. Ronnie had confided in him and told him that he was absolutely terrified as he could not swim.

Alas, Ronnie did not make it to the one lifeboat. He ended up in the sea and subsequently drowned.

"Oh Lord, me thought what pain it was to drown," that quotation from Richard III immediately springs to mind.

Grandfather was so grateful to Mr Livingstone that he offered him a job as a manager of one of his cinemas.

Alas, that did not work out well, and Mr Livingstone eventually left grandfather's employment in less than happy circumstances.

Able Seaman William Holden Anderson was badly wounded in the shelling of *HMS Yin Ping*. His leg was broken, and he received a large number of shrapnel wounds. He was highly commended by Lieutenant Wilkinson for the manner in which he carried out his duties. He was captured, but it is not certain where he spent his captivity, nor is it known whether he actually survived his captivity, and, if he did survive, what happened to him after the war.

Maurice William Arthur Bentley was captured on Bangka Island two days after successfully surviving the sinking.

Stokers R. Hodgson and C. Hughes also made it to Bangka Island where they were captured. They were both listed as POWs at Muntok and then Palembang.

Able Seaman Jack Ellis of Heckmondwike, Yorkshire, and Able Seaman James Walker of Balornock, Glasgow, were the only two crew members unaccounted for, and it is assumed that they both lost their lives when *HMS Yin Ping* sank.

Petty Officer Charles Simpson made it to Muntok on Bangka Island, where he was captured and eventually imprisoned in Palembang.

Able Seaman Arthur Henry Keen, born in Blackpool in December 1913, had a varied career. He had started his working life as an able seaman with the Cunard White Star Line. He then worked as a rigger and dock labourer in Liverpool before joining *HMS Repulse* in August 1939. He survived the sinking of the *Repulse* and was posted to *HMS Sultan*, the naval shore base in Singapore. It is not clear whether he was part of the crew of *HMS Yin Ping*, or another escapee. It is not known what happened to him.

E.R. Jones, a former crew member on the *Repulse,* managed to escape in the RAF launch with Captain Chapman and Lieutenant Wilkinson. He was subsequently listed as a POW at both Muntok and Palembang, as the launch was eventually captured by the

Japanese.

Stoker Seaman Dennis McCarthy, born in 1916, managed a similar escape route on the RAF launch, only to end up in captivity as well.

Petty Officer McFarling was born in 1904. Whilst living in North Gosforth, Newcastle Upon Tyne, he enlisted even though he was only 17. He had been on the *Eureka*, the launch towed by *HMS Yin Ping* before it sank.

He, along with several others, made it to Bangka Island, where he was captured. He survived his captivity at Muntok, Palembang, Changi and Kranji. After the war, he became a fish fryer in Northumberland.

Along with Petty Officer McFarling and the others who had been on the *Eureka*, Able Seaman Nicholls landed on Bangka Island, but thereafter what happened to him is a mystery, his name not appearing in any of the POW camps.

AC/LAC William Taffy Yates, born in 1922, a volunteer with the RAFVR, survived the sinking of *HMS Yin Ping*. He was captured and held for three days at Muntok. He was then transferred to Palembang and from there to Sungei Ron from where he was released in July 1945. He eventually died aged 65 in Dyfed, Cardiganshire.

Destined to lose his life was Mechanic Second Class Robert Silcock. He was 27, and originally came from Oakworth in Yorkshire. He left a wife Irene in Plymouth, from where he had set sail on the *Prince of Wales*. He had been a mechanic on the *Eureka* launch, and is commemorated on the Plymouth Naval Memorial.

Signalman Arthur Donald Scott, aged 26 from Auckland, also perished on *HMS Yin Ping*, but other than that little is known about him.

LAC/AC Harold Francis, another RAFVR volunteer, came from Worcester. It is probable, but by no means certain, that he was, like my uncle Ronnie, a passenger and intending escapee on *HMS Yin*

Ping. His fate is unknown.

Petty Officer Simpson managed to clamber on to the lifeboat and, like many others, ended up in Muntok.

Another RAFVR volunteer, Leslie Kenneth Hill, is listed as possibly being aboard *HMS Yin Ping*, but other sources suggest he died on the *HMS Empire Star*, when it was hit by a torpedo and sunk with the loss of 42 lives.

One of the heroes of the sinking of *HMS Yin Ping* was Lieutenant Patrick Ormond Howard Wilkinson, *HMS Yin Ping* captain.

As we know, his wife Alice had been given permission to be on board. Unfortunately, she had been killed when the first Japanese salvo struck *HMS Yin Ping*'s bridge.

Lieutenant Wilkinson was one of the last to abandon ship when it was clear that *HMS Yin Ping* was about to sink.

He had been wounded when the bridge was first struck, but this did not deter him from doing everything that he could to assist his passengers and crew.

He organised the launch of the one serviceable lifeboat, helping to right it when it capsized and arranging for it to be occupied by the wounded, whilst able-bodied men, including himself, swam alongside until they were picked up by a Japanese captured RAF launch.

As well as being wounded, he would have been in deep shock at the loss of his wife.

He was taken to Muntok, where he remained until some time in March, when he was moved to Palembang. In September, he was moved to an orientation camp, and then to Sungei where he remained for a year.

In May 1945, he was transferred to Changi in Singapore, and there he stayed until the Japanese surrendered in September 1945.

On release, he came back to England and lived for a time in

Bournemouth. He later remarried, and in 1946 went back to Singapore. He eventually died in Queensland in 1976. Whilst he was incarcerated, he wrote a full report of the sinking of *HMS Yin Ping*, which has proved invaluable to this author.

Arthur McKenzie was on *HMS Yin Ping*. He was born in 1919 in Liverpool and his extraordinary story is available on YouTube.

Arthur joined the RAF in 1938 and after a series of postings he eventually found himself in Singapore being hustled on to the *HMS Trang*. It is probable that he at least spoke to Ronnie, maybe even sitting next to him. Perhaps they helped each other when they were transferred from *HMS Trang* to *HMS Yin Ping*.

Arthur estimated that there were 52 ships of varying types leaving Singapore of which 48 were shelled, sunk or captured. In the chaos of the time it is not surprising that estimates of the numbers of the evacuation fleet varied, as Arthur's estimate differed from the figures already given.

When *HMS Yin Ping* came under fire from the *Sendai*, Arthur remembered how the first shell missed its target. The second shell hit the starboard side, where many of the men were watching the action and most were tragically wiped out. The third shell set the ship on fire. This was followed by a fourth shell which hit below deck and thus sank the boat.

Following the sinking, Arthur found himself in the water. Out of self-preservation he started to swim. Initially, he had a companion, the ship's cook, but they soon lost contact with each other.

Arthur, not knowing exactly where he was going, allowed himself to be carried by the tide. He was in the sea for 48 hours. Luckily, he found a child's cork life jacket and a mattress floating in the sea and these helped him to maintain buoyancy. Eventually, he felt land beneath his feet and he stepped on to a beach on Bangka Island.

He was emaciated, totally exhausted and deaf from the shelling of *HMS Yin Ping*, and with shrapnel in his shoulder. He was almost dying of thirst, as the only sustenance he had had for two days had been the inside of an onion which he found floating in the sea. Luckily, he landed on a relatively safe part of Bangka Island, and was initially helped by some local Chinese, who gave him a pair of trousers and a cotton shirt, and guided him into the shade and looked after him. After two days, he clearly needed medical attention and therefore wandered down the beach in search of a Japanese to whom he could surrender. Arthur was lucky in that the Japanese to whom he surrendered did not kill him, as had happened to so many other survivors. By this time he was in a sad medical condition weighing only 6 ½ stone. He was given medical attention and then transferred to Muntok POW camp, then Palembang, then Changi.

Eventually, he was transferred to Taiwan to work in a stone quarry. He ended up in Sendai in Japan working in the shipyard, arriving home on 5th September 1945.

Arthur's story, a remarkable survival story, was reinforced by his strong Christian faith. He eventually married a local Liverpool girl and, in 2019, with his large family he joyously celebrated his hundredth birthday.

Finally, the story of LAC Eric Shepherd RAF needs to be told in some detail as an example of what so many survivors went through and as a tribute to his extraordinary resilience. He is a link between the sinking of *HMS Yin Ping* and what happened on Bangka Island. Aged 19 at the time of the Japanese invasion, he had been an RAF driver and one of 250 RAF men put on seven different evacuation vessels. Apparently six of those vessels were sunk and only 45 men out of the 250 reached some sort of safety.

His recollection of the shelling and sinking of *HMS Yin Ping* was that without warning, three shells hit the ship, the first in the forward well deck, where most men were located, the second hit the bridge, and the third hit the aft port side. He was located in the aft, but survived and abandoned ship with others. He thought 25 out of 75 survived the sinking. He managed to swim to a life raft and joined around 16 to 20 other men hanging on around its edge. During that night many of those men drowned or died through exhaustion and of their wounds. By morning there were only eight, including Eric, left around the raft. They managed to climb on to it and balance it by sitting two men along each edge.

A Japanese destroyer made two pass-bys after the sinking, and machine gunned their raft, as was expected. They survived by getting underneath the raft, and then somehow climbing back aboard and re-boarding the vessel. Sometime the following afternoon an RAF air sea rescue launch under the command of Sergeant Macdonald picked up the survivors, including Eric. The launch had already been captured by the Japanese but was allowed to pick up survivors and was running on reduced power on one engine. They were taken to and landed on a jetty on Bangka Island at Muntok. Most of them had only a shirt on for clothing, as they had discarded their trousers, jackets, and shoes. in order to stay afloat by lessening their weight, and to avoid being dragged down. From the jetty they were taken to a local prison for a very short time, then taken on to the local airfield. The airfield had been sabotaged by the local Dutch forces by digging trenches 10ft wide and 8ft deep across the runway. They were all lined up with their backs to the trenches, and machine guns were placed at intervals opposite them. The plan appeared to be a mass killing.

They were fortunate that the senior officer present was Air Commodore C.O.F. Modin, whose statement of events is available in the National Archives. After prolonged negotiation with the Japanese officer, it was agreed that they would fill in the trenches in return for their lives. It was an offer they could not refuse. They were set to work straight away. At this point they were all exhausted, hungry, thirsty and frightened, having come straight from the sea, with no clothes or footwear. Work continued night and day for between three days to a week. At night, the Japanese surrounded the trenches with their vehicles, with headlights turned on, so that work could continue. They were given their first food on the second day and had also been given water. When the work was complete, they were returned to the local prison in the main town of Muntok, where they slept on sacks of peppercorns.

In April 1942, Eric was moved to Palembang where he was placed in Charitas Hospital with malaria, dysentery and beriberi –

the latter causing paralysis of his legs for the next 12 months, before undergoing surgery by the impressive Dutch doctor in Palembang camp, Dr Pieter Tekelenburg. He was later arrested and tortured by the Japanese secret police, the Kempeitai, and died just before the end of the war. Eric returned to Chung Wha camp on crutches and was then later sent to Sungei Ron camp, where starvation, disease and sickness were rife, and deaths were common. He survived the war, weighing just under five stone when liberated.

Eric later made the observation that *HMS Yin Ping* was an obvious target, due to the fact that it was carrying a very senior naval captain, and flying the full massive flag of his rank. This flag almost dwarfed the size of *HMS Yin Ping*, looked ridiculous and advertised the fact that the ship was carrying someone ready to do battle!

To make *HMS Yin Ping* an even easier target, running lights were left on all the time. The reason for this will never be known. The attack took place at dusk, and had there been no lights the Japanese would have had difficulty in picking out *HMS Yin Ping* as, at that time, they had not developed radar for use on their ships.

So why did *HMS Yin Ping* in particular come to meet its fate? Like many of the vessels destroyed at that time, it was delayed by the order to stop and help other ships and launches which had run aground or had mechanical problems.

In hindsight, *HMS Yin Ping* should not have followed orders, nor should she have sheltered in the many islands of the Rhio Archipelago during the day. She could perhaps have escaped, had she just ploughed on to her intended destination.

If she had simply left Singapore and headed straight for Batavia, she would have arrived on 15th February, as did *HMS Scott Harley*, a slow coal-burning auxiliary minesweeper, whose captain disobeyed orders to hide up during the day. She simply plodded on at a steady six knots, eventually reaching safety.

As with the other evacuation ships, *HMS Yin Ping* was unable to learn of the Japanese warships lying in wait in the Bangka Strait, because the British officer responsible for radio/morse code in Singapore had jumped the gun and destroyed his codebooks prematurely, so no messages could be sent or received.

A further devastating coincidence meant that any survivors reaching Bangka Island would do so at the same time as one of the most brutal Japanese regiments, the 229th, which had been responsible for some of the terrible massacres in Hong Kong.

11. THE KILLINGS ON BANGKA ISLAND

Much has been written about the massacre on 16th February 1942 of approximately 83 civilians, Australian nurses and servicemen on Radji Beach, Bangka Island, a relatively small island some 382 miles east of Sumatra and 20 miles from where *HMS Yin Ping* sank. It is not so well-known perhaps that there were many other separate killings on that island at the same time.

The connection with *HMS Yin Ping* comes in the form of affidavit evidence from Corporal Robert Henry Seddon, a *Yin Ping* survivor.

Born in 1918, he was serving in the Royal Marines and, like many others, was attempting to escape Singapore.

He was manning a Lewis gun at the time the ship sank. He could not get into the lifeboat and so started to swim, not knowing exactly where he was going.

About 5 pm the day after the sinking, he managed to swim close to Bangka Island. When he was about 100 yards from the shore, he saw a number of people on the beach: Japanese soldiers, English soldiers, some civilian men and women and several nurses.

"The Japs appeared to be rounding them up and were pushing them with rifles with fixed bayonets. They sorted them into three rows in separate parts of the beach, but close together. The party on the right, mostly civilian women and some civilian men (apparently old men), were marched about a mile along the beach and disappeared. The other two groups turned to face the sea, it looked as though they were ordered to by the Japs. The centre group were all women, mostly nurses. The left-hand group were all men. After they turned, I waved and shouted. One of the nurses saw me and waved to me, I thought that she meant me to keep down and out of sight. Two or three men and women made a break for it into the water. One was shot but kept on swimming away from the beach to sea. Of the other two, one was bayoneted at the waist. The remaining men and women who were trying to escape were bayoneted and shot.

I was eventually washed on to the beach and collapsed about two hundred yards along from the Japs. I was trying to see what was going on but was too weak to move. Two Japs had seen me. One with a rifle and sword kicked me. The other one with just a sword flicked me under both arms. I was too exhausted to move at all. I think they considered I was dead. They moved off along the beach. A few hours later I crawled up the beach to find some fresh water and drank enough to get into the jungle."

Later that day, he came across Seaman Wilding from the *HMS Li Wo*, which had also been sunk, and a Malay sailor from that ship. Next morning all three of them returned to the beach and saw bodies left where they had been killed. He also came across Stoker Lloyd from the *SS Vyner Brooke*, who had been amongst those shot on the beach, but who had swum out to sea and survived the massacre.

It is not clear how many survivors were from *HMS Yin Ping*, the *Tandjong Penang*, the *Vyner Brooke*, the *Siang Wo*, the *Li Wo*, and the *Pulo Soegi*, all of which had been sunk nearby in the Bangka Strait.

Apparently, this is what had happened:

On the morning of 16th February, a disparate group had gathered on Radji Beach, terrified, bewildered, hungry and wet.

During the early part of that morning, the first officer of the *Vyner Brooke*, Lieutenant Bill Sedgeman RNR, had gone in search of the Japanese to advise that the group on the beach wanted to surrender.

A little later, a group of 15 servicemen set off independently for Muntok, also determined to surrender.

This left approximately 100 people on the beach, about 22 Australian army nurses, three New Zealand naval officers, a mixed group of 55 British civilians, soldiers, sailors and other survivors from various ships, as well as nurses from the *Vyner Brooke*.

Included in this group were several small children and teenagers. Many in the group were badly burned or wounded, some lying on makeshift stretchers. Many had been on the beach for 36 hours without food, with only a little water from a stream they had found. It is this group that we are most concerned with.

It seems that Corporal Seddon did not actually witness the terrible events which are now so well known. He had merely seen some random killings and the lining up of the various groups, and only later observed the tragic results of the slaughter.

Apparently, Lieutenant Sedgeman had located some Japanese soldiers and appraised them of the situation, confirming the desire of the group to surrender. He returned to the beach, with 20 or so Japanese soldiers, who immediately ordered half of the men to stand, and then marched them, at bayonet point, down to a secluded part of the beach and out of sight of the remaining groups.

A few moments later the Japanese returned, gathered the remaining men and forced them to march down the same path. This left the 22 nurses and an elderly woman who had asked to stay behind to look after her wounded husband.

On each occasion, the sounds of gunshots were distinctly heard by those left on the beach.

Eventually, the Japanese returned holding rifles and bayonets that were dripping with fresh blood. They sat in front of the nurses and cleaned their weapons. Once that was done they ordered the women, mainly nurses, to line up knee-high in the surf all facing the horizon in a straight line.

They did so without a murmur, without tears or cries.

Matron Irene Drummond tried to rally them saying, "chin up girls. I'm proud of you and love you all."

They were then ordered to march into the sea. When they got waist deep, the Japanese opened fire on them with a machine gun. One by one the nurses fell, some on top of each other, the sea red with their blood.

The only survivor of this massacre was Nurse Vivian Bullwinkel, whose story can be readily accessed online.

Very briefly, she was shot several times, but knew instinctively that her wounds were not fatal. She held her breath as the Japanese walked into the surf, bayoneting anyone they still deemed to be alive.

As she lay immobile, the current slowly washed her ashore. She lay on the beach, not daring to move, until nightfall. In due course, she levered herself up and observing that there was no one on the beach. She somehow found her way into the forest fringing the beach, where she collapsed. She eventually found a spring from which she drank gratefully. At the same time, she came across a wounded British soldier, Private Pat Kingsley, who had survived the massacre of the men by the Japanese.

They looked after each other for 12 days, until they finally decided that they could not survive any longer. After celebrating Private Kingsley's 39th birthday, on 28th February, they eventually surrendered at Muntok.

Shortly afterwards, Private Kingsley died from his wounds in the men's camp. Vivian Bullwinkel was to remain a prisoner of the Japanese for the next three-and-a-half years. As the only surviving witness of the massacre, she had to keep her knowledge secret, otherwise she would most certainly have been killed.

In the end she survived her captivity to give evidence at a War Crimes Tribunal.

There is also the dark story of the rape of the nurses before they were killed. Apparently, Vivian Bullwinkel was forbidden to give evidence about this at the War Crimes Tribunal, and the story of this abomination only came out in 2019, after much research.

Confirmation of the massacre came in Robert Henry Seddon's affidavit. Following a night in the jungle by the beach, next morning – 17th February, "I searched around and found the bodies: 15 New Zealand and Australian nursing sisters, 15 British service personnel and five merchant seaman, probably crewmembers. I walked further along the beach and found two more lifeboats grounded and nearby the bodies of seven RN personnel. The latter included two officers and the whole party appear to have been shot and bayoneted." It must be assumed that there were other bodies which had been carried out to sea or were lying unnoticed in the surf.

Robert Henry Seddon was eventually captured and became a POW in Muntok, followed by Palembang. He survived his wartime captivity and returned home to Lincolnshire, where he eventually died in 2003. He was buried in Saint Nicholas Churchyard, Haxey, near Scunthorpe.

The group of servicemen who left Radji Beach before the Japanese arrived had assisted the wounded survivors by lighting fires and cooking for them, but had then decided to head to Muntok. En route, they met a squad of Japanese soldiers who attacked them. One of the survivors, Leading Seaman Victor Spencer, who had been left for dead, says that he had regained consciousness after being bayoneted to find that all the others in his group had been killed. He eventually made it to Muntok accompanied by another Radji Beach survivor, Leading Seaman Bruce Hadley, who unfortunately died of his wounds soon after.

It is not known exactly how many died in the dreadful Radji Beach massacre, and in other places of the island.

In due course, a memorial plaque commemorating the massacre was erected on the beach. On 16th February 2019, a memorial service was held on the beautiful beach where such atrocities had been carried out.

The address was given by Michael Pether, born in Singapore

soon after the war. His parents were a British father, who had spent the war as an internee in Changi Prison, and a New Zealand mother, who had been evacuated back to New Zealand at Christmas 1941 after the Japanese started bombing Singapore

His maternal grandparents and a young 19-year-old uncle were also in Singapore when the Japanese landed on Singapore Island.

His grandfather became an internee, and his grandmother managed to escape to Batavia. However, his young uncle was killed by the Japanese whilst attempting to escape.

Michael has spent much of his life outside work in researching the 100 or so vessels (i.e. those ships in the 'official' fleet and the many others which joined unofficially in the hope of gaining some protection) which attempted to flee Singapore. So far, he has completed 26 individual memorial documents, including *HMS Yin Ping*, out of the 80 vessels which were sunk, scuttled or captured.

Without Michael's research, this part of the book would not have been possible, and I thank him.

In Memory Of

Leading Aircraftman

FRANCIS RONALD EMERY

Service Number: 1053493

Royal Air Force Volunteer Reserve who died on 15 February 1942 Age 29

Son of James Frederick and Florence Beatrice Emery, of Poulton-le-Fylde, Lancashire.

Remembered with Honour

SINGAPORE MEMORIAL

Column 416.

COMMONWEALTH
WAR GRAVES

COMMEMORATED IN PERPETUITY BY THE COMMONWEALTH
WAR GRAVES COMMISSION

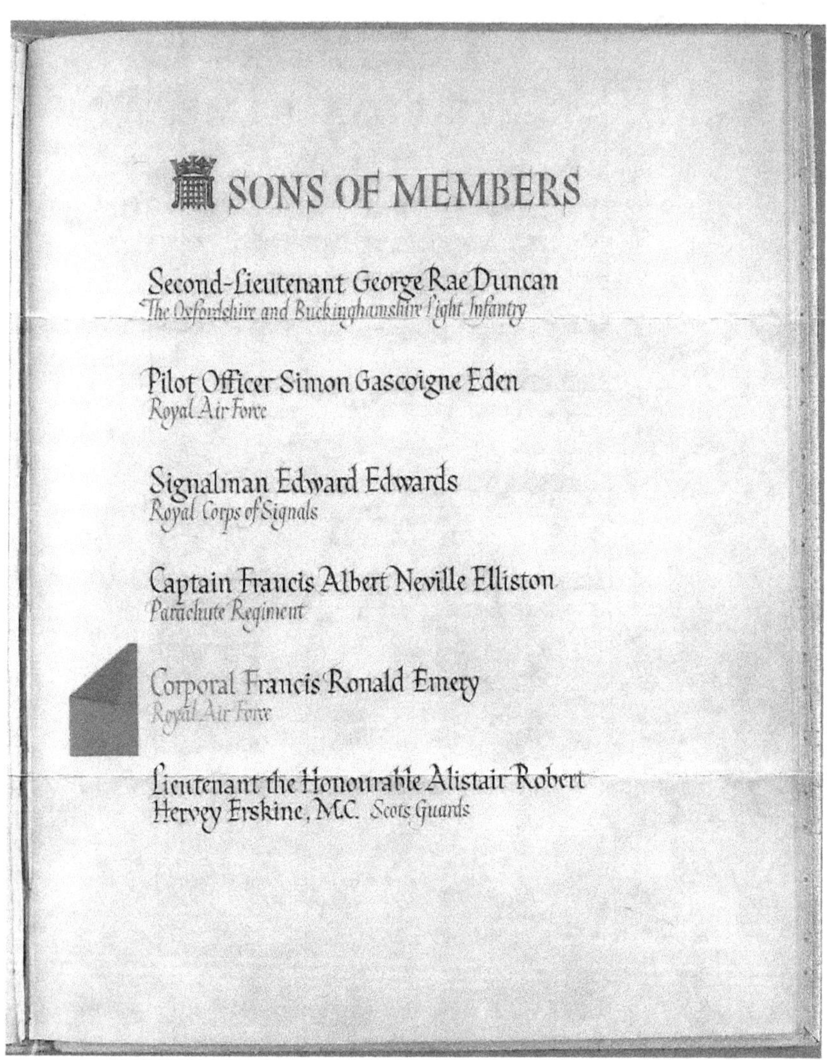

Memorial in the Houses of Parliament

12. REFLECTIONS

So that was the story of *HMS Yin Ping*, a story not much different from those of the many ships of various types and sizes which left Singapore in their mad dash for freedom, only for most of them to meet the same terrible fate.

So many lives lost, so many futures ruined, so many families prostrate with grief.

My parents and grandparents were no different from the many hundreds of families who suffered in the same way.

Who knows what Ronnie would have achieved, what children he would have had, what joy he would have brought to others?

However, it is no use pretending that Ronnie's loss was of any greater or lesser importance than anyone else's. Of course, when it is one's own family's suffering, the pain is that much worse.

Ronnie suffered the agony and panic of drowning, but who is to say that mode of death is any better or worse than waiting in line with others to be bayoneted?

All such terrible, almost indescribable tragedies.

So the years roll by. As I write this, the 80th anniversary of the debacle of the flight from Singapore has passed. The sinking of so many ships, the loss of so many lives are but memories. I am no longer a little lad riding on Uncle Ronnie's shoulders.

Maybe on the seabed of the Bangka Strait there will be some vestiges of Ronnie and so many others, all resting in peace, the waves above them heading for Bangka Island, to wash away the remains of others from that terrible time, long ago.

Francis Ronald Emery, RAFVR (Service Number 1053493) is commemorated and remembered with honour on the Singapore War Memorial Column 416.

May he, along with others everywhere, rest in peace.

COMMEMORATIVE ADDRESS RADJI BEACH 16 FEBRUARY 2019 delivered at Tin Museum, Muntok by Michael Pether and reproduced with his kind permission

Today we remember the eighty or so people whose lives were taken near this spot on the morning of 16th February 1942 - and, importantly, the many others who were killed by the Japanese during the surrounding days up and down this peaceful coastline from Tanjung Kilian to Tanjung Genting. The connection between those who died and those who are here today is perhaps a bond of respect, empathy and family love - those whose lives were taken had just minutes to contemplate what was about to occur. Almost certainly, their thoughts included those they held most dear and a fervent hope they would be remembered, possibly even someone would search for them. They would not have wanted to die alone. May I suggest that for us to empathise with their final life experiences, which were even more profoundly traumatising than most people realise, it may help to understand what had been happening in their lives in previous months and days. If I take you back, and we had we had been able to see Malaya (or even parts of Singapore) from the air in early December 1941 we would have seen a beautiful undulating patchwork of wild green jungle, orderly rows of rubber trees, peaceful prosperous busy towns interlaced with muddy brown rivers, tumbling cool streams and black tar sealed roads - this was the world of the people who were later washed ashore on Bangka Island. However, on the 8th December 1941 that peaceful patchwork was torn and the very fabric of life, of every ethnicity, began to be literally put through the shredding machine that was the invading Japanese army. Hundreds of thousands of people were dislocated and began retreating to the anticipated safety of Singapore. By the 11th February 1942, only eight weeks after the first shots were fired, the marauding Japanese troops were well advanced across Singapore Island and chaos had developed in that bombed and burning city. In particular, a new fear had spread for the safety of all remaining women and the nurses stationed across the hospitals and aid posts on the Island. News of the atrocities inflicted by the 229th Infantry Division of the Japanese army on the European and Chinese nurses at St Stephens Hospital in Hong Kong on Christmas Eve 1941 had finally reached Singapore. An urgent order was given to evacuate all remaining nurses, key army personnel and, where possible, civilian women and children, and to clear Singapore Harbour of all remaining ships. As a result, some sixty vessels of hugely varying size and shape left Singapore during the last few days before the Surrender to the Japanese on 15th February 1942 - at least 40 to 50 of these would be attacked and sunk before they reached the safety of Batavia (now Jakarta).

Only 10 to 15 of these ships would make it to safety through the Bangka Straits, but a similar number would be sunk within sight of where we stand today. Why did this awful tragedy at sea happen? Because someone in command ordered the evacuation ships to travel only by night, and during the day to try and 'hide' amongst the myriad of islands of the Rhio Archipelago - the harsh reality was that those Captains who simply ignored those orders and steamed without stopping were the ones whose ships survived; almost every ship which took shelter delayed their journey with the result that they fell into the range of arriving Japanese Navy warships and Japanese bombers. Also, the last days of the evacuation coincided with the arrival in these waters of the huge Japanese invasion force on troop ships bound for Sumatra and accompanied by a flotilla of very modern, heavily armed and fast Japanese warships. Also, the Royal Navy radio code books, which would have allowed decoding of the warning messages from earlier evacuation ships as to the arrival of Japanese warships in the evacuation route, had been either destroyed or removed prematurely from Singapore by the time the last ships were leaving. Finally, for those who would later look for refuge on Bangka Island, a terrible twist of fate had ordained that the same evil men of the Headquarters Companies from the 229th Infantry Regiment of the Japanese Army, who had violated and murdered the nurses in Hong Kong, had been assigned to invade and hold Bangka. So, by 'Black Friday', i.e. Friday 13th February 1942, whilst ships were still leaving Singapore Harbour, the Japanese Navy and Airforce had reached the seas and islands behind me - they effectively controlled the horizon as far as your eye can see. Some of the first evacuees to be attacked by Japanese warships in this broad area were those on the auxiliary merchant ship '*Giang Bee*' on the night of 13th February - of the 300 women, children and men on board, some 200 would die in the shelling and sinking of the ship. The first of the only two lifeboats to be successfully launched and reach land with fifty-six people on board would beach north of here at Djaboes two days later - they were fortunate, they would land about the same time as the infamous 229th Infantry Regiment reached the south coast of the island. The occupants of the other lifeboat would later be landed at Muntok under controlled circumstances, after being rescued by '*HMS Tapah*'.

The next day, Saturday 14th February, at 1.30pm in the afternoon the '*SS Vyner Brooke*' - carrying around 250 women (including the sixty-five Australian Army Nurses) and what also has become apparent, a large group of children, plus a smaller number of civilian men and servicemen - was attacked by Japanese bombers whilst racing towards the Bangka Straits from Pulau Tujuh (or Kepulan Tujuh). It sank about 10 km off Tanjung Betumpah. Later that evening and well into the night two lifeboats ground ashore along 'Radji Beach' carrying twenty-one of the Australian Army nurses and another forty or so civilian women, children, and men plus ships' crew and several military personnel. It is calculated that over half those that boarded the '*Vyner Brooke*' in Singapore died during the attack, the sinking, or in the sea struggling towards land and on Radji Beach, not to mention the others who would later die from malnutrition, disease and physical abuse in the horrendous internment camps of southern Sumatra. By Sunday 15th February, just after dawn, the Japanese Navy ships were well established, lying in wait across the northern entrance to the Bangka Straits. As the sun began to rise, they located two small Royal Navy patrol vessels of wood construction - *ML311* and *ML433*. As the heavy high explosive shells tore apart these lightweight craft, some sixty crew and army personnel passengers would die, firstly on *ML311*, and then a similar number on *ML433*. Survivors, many badly wounded, swam towards Bangka island (a few towards Sumatra) and either death or prison camp. Later that Sunday, just after dusk and about thirty-two kilometres north of Muntok lighthouse, the Japanese destroyers located and opened fire on the naval tugboat '*HMS Yin Ping*' carrying naval personnel evacuees, and within minutes some fifty people lost their lives. Of the twenty-six or so survivors who reached shore, some would be taken prisoner at Muntok, whilst others reached the western coats of Bangka and struggled ashore late on the morning of 16th February - a few would then bear witness to the horrors of what had already occurred at Radji Beach and themselves feel the pain of a Japanese bayonet thrust! Finally, that Sunday, around midnight, the Auxiliary patrol vessel '*Pulo Soegi*', carrying a large contingent of selected skilled men from the Royal Army Ordnance Corps entered the Bangka Straits only to encounter the Japanese warships which opened fire. This small wooden coastal trader was shattered and burning within minutes - almost sixty men were killed. Of the twenty five surviving crew and RAOC men, a few strong swimmers managed to reboard the burning and sinking vessel and launch a small lifeboat in which they headed towards a beach where they saw the remnants of a bonfire. Twenty men in that lifeboat would arrive at Radji Beach next morning with hope they had reached safety.

As dawn broke on Monday 16th February the carnage at sea continued - the little launch '*Elizabeth*' (designated as a 'tugboat') and with almost thirty men on board - was intercepted by the Japanese destroyers in the Bangka Straits and sunk by shellfire - the twenty-three survivors struck out, swimming for the coast of Bangka island - a few for Sumatra. We know two survivors reached small islands near Bangka within a couple of days and then Bangka Island itself - only to be captured. The other twenty-one survivors of the sinking were never heard of again - some of these were young, very fit and uninjured men from the elite Royal Marines, so it leaves us with the haunting question of whether they all lost their lives in the sea or at the hands of the Japanese once they reached the coast of this island? So, that Monday morning of 16th February 1942, gathered on 'Radji Beach' were about 100 people - survivors of the *'Vyner Brooke'*, the *'Pulo Soegi'* and, it appears, subject to further research, possibly even another vessel. This group comprised small children, teenagers, mothers and wives, a small group of civilian men, Australian Army nurses and a sizeable group of servicemen comprising ships' officers, ships' crew and RAOC soldiers, many very badly burned, and wounded and lying on makeshift stretchers under the nearby trees and in a fisherman's hut. By then most had been on the beach for thirty-six hours with little in the way of food and only the water from a small stream they had found. The situation was untenable and the decision was made by Lt Bill Sedgeman, the senior officer of the *'Vyner Brooke'*, and Matron Irene Drummond to send firstly the 'walking wounded' servicemen, who would be no help in carrying stretchers, and then the uninjured civilian women and children, under the care of several older civilian men in groups, to begin the trek through the jungle towards Muntok. This action saved the lives of probably some twenty-five or more people and most of them would go on to survive the rigours of internment and POW camps. If there is one small shaft of positive light from this terrible day, it is the fact that one of that group trudging along jungle paths to Muntok was a little three year old boy by the name of Isidore Warman - his father had died during the sinking of the *'Vyner Brooke'* and his mother would also pass away from pneumonia within two weeks of internment, leaving him alone in the world - but Isidore, known as 'Mischa' to other internees during the War, survived all these horrors and all the coming hardships and is today a retired accountant and contented grandfather in Florida, USA.

Soon after their departure, the remaining survivors on Radji Beach, lying wounded on stretchers or busy preparing to surrender to the Japanese and make the same trek to Muntok, saw Lt Bill Sedgeman and two sailors, who had gone to search for the Japanese and let them know that this unarmed group wished to surrender, return and emerge from the jungle track, followed by a Japanese officer carrying a sword and around twenty heavily armed Japanese troops. These were the troops from the two companies of the 229th Infantry division who had landed on Bangka Island the previous day. We now know that this Japanese officer, whose name I will not speak but who was in command of the invasion force, had immediately, upon arrival on Bangka, given the order to his men that they were to summarily kill all shipwrecked survivors found on the beaches of the Island. The soldiers - as Japanese troops had repeated countless of times since invading China in the mid1930s and throughout their campaign in Malaya - immediately began to separate the officers (it appears excluding Sedgeman) from the naval ratings and ordinary soldiers so as to gain control over a group that clearly outnumbered them three to one. These senior men were then taken south along the beach over the small headland and the incomprehensible savagery by the Japanese began. The details and events of that morning of infamy are now well documented - men and women bayoneted, shot and cut down where they stood. The wounded lying on makeshift stretchers and in the fisherman's hut bayoneted where they lay, the lives of some nurses even being taken as they knelt trying to tend to the wounds of the men who were dying from the first murderous onslaught by the Japanese troops. At least half the people killed on Radji Beach remain anonymous, but further research in recent months has taken us closer to learning who lost their lives that day. It has moved us to a new clearer understanding of the identities of the British who died and has brought new understanding that the toll included New Zealanders. Today we are able to speak the names of others whose lives were brutally taken - in addition to the names of the noble women of the Australian Army Nursing service and the servicemen and civilians we are already able to honour individually. We now 'Bring in from the Cold', so to speak: At Radji Beach , Lt Arthur John Waller Martin - known as 'Peter' - of the Royal New Zealand Naval Volunteer Reserve, Captain of the aforementioned *'Pulo Soegi'* and latterly from Auckland, New Zealand. Lt Leonard Stephen Day, also of the *'Pulo Soegi'* and the Malayan Royal Naval Volunteer Reserve.

Another, as yet not specifically unidentified, Lieutenant of the Royal New Zealand Naval Volunteer Reserve and a similarly yet to be individually identified Officer of the Royal Naval Volunteer

Reserve and from the RAOC complement on the '*Pulo Soegi*', Craftsman Arnold Wilson Atkins of the Royal Army Ordnance Corps, from Dewsbury, Yorkshire and Sergeant Robert George Hurrell, Royal Army Ordnance Corps from Hinckley, Leicestershire. There are several other specific men of the RAOC who - it is becoming more clear - were also on Radji Beach that day, but we do not have sufficient evidence at this stage to certainly state that they lost their lives specifically during this massacre. As mentioned already, many others lost their lives at the hands of the Japanese up and down the west coast of Bangka Island as they reached land from their sunken ships and we take this opportunity to today remember; Lt Basil Shaw, Royal New Zealand Naval Volunteer Reserve, Captain of the '*SS Tandjong Pinang*' and from the Hawkes Bay in New Zealand and Able Seaman Oswald Littlewood Young, Royal Navy, from County Durham, England. Both were murdered by the Japanese near Tanjung Oelar after rowing for several days in a small dinghy to Bangka Island to seek help for those still in the sea from their sunken ship. Today they lie in a grave at Kranji War Cemetery in Singapore. I also ask today that, now and in the future, we take time to remember those other men and women, numbering in the dozens, who survived the sinking of their ships and courageously struggled to what appeared to be the welcoming shores of Bangka Island - as they most surely did - but were then also murdered without trace on the beaches to the north and south along this coast. Please understand - these beaches in February 1942 became the last resting place for the remains of literally hundreds, I repeat hundreds, of evacuees from Singapore who lost their lives as a result of the attacks and sinking of their evacuation ship - which had, only a day or two before, offered them so much hope. To be blunt, for years after and even when, in 1946, the Allied War Graves Parties came to Bangka Island to try and make sense of what had occurred, the bones of those hundreds of innocent human beings were starkly evident on these pristine beaches. Those bones remain there to this day and in that context this western coastline of Bangka Island is Hallowed Ground. May they forever rest in peace in this beautiful place on this distant shore.

PART THREE

CAPTIVITY

INTRODUCTION

We now have to leave the tragic tales of the ships and personnel trying to escape the hell that was Singapore.

The fleet was scattered, most ships sunk. Many crew and passengers had been killed in awful circumstances, some had drowned, some had been captured.

Of course, BB and the thousands of other civilian and military internees and prisoners could not possibly know the disaster that had befallen the escaping flotilla.

Later, a few of them would learn about the tragedy from those who were captured at sea or on Bangka Island, as eventually some of those survivors would be sent to the various POW camps in which BB and his fellow soldiers were destined to be incarcerated.

They would have heard terrible stories about awful events.

There have, of course, been a considerable number of books written about the plight of the many POWs in Japanese hands – the torture, the cruelty and the executions, as well as the day-to-day exhausting work routines, forced upon sick and emaciated prisoners.

There have also been many personal memoirs, exhibitions, documentaries and lectures. Memorials have been erected, and pilgrimages undertaken.

This part of the book does not make any attempt to cover the lengthy and tragic story of the majority of the POWs, and only brief details of the camps will be given.

As has been said, this is one man's story of a time when all had to suffer and so, by extension, it is the story of the survivors of his regiment, the 137, who, in the main, were imprisoned together. Many of them suffered much more than BB; some suffered less and, of course, there were those who, sadly, did not survive at all.

Certain charismatic personalities, who were outstanding characters and leaders, will also be mentioned. This is not to denigrate or insult the memories of the thousands of POWs who receive no mention at all, but who are, in effect, the main part and purpose of the overall story.

13. FIRST STAGES OF CAPTIVITY

On 18th June 1942, BB was uprooted from imprisonment in Changi and transported some 1,150 miles to Siam (now Thailand) as part of a forward contingent of some 3,000 men under the command of Major R.S. (Paddy) Sykes of 18th Infantry Division.

Their destination was Ban Pong, a village and POW camp adjacent to a Buddhist monastery, where Major Sykes was to be the first British Camp Commander. In that capacity he was one of the first to receive communication from the V Organisation. He was worried that the note was a plot, but after consultation with his fellow officers he replied, thus establishing the connection with the V Organisation, and Boon Pong.

The V Organisation, founded in Bangkok, secretly smuggled money and medicines to several camps along the railway and did whatever it could to frustrate the Japanese war efforts. Boon Pong (of whom more later) was one of the agents.

The official post-war report on the V Organisation paid tribute to Paddy Sykes as the instigator and organiser of the scheme in Thailand.

His conduct, fearlessness and clear-sighted policies were the foundations of the Organisation's success.

As will be seen later, BB made contact with Boon Pong and received many communications from the V Organisation.

In due course, it became clear that the POWs were there to act as labourers in the construction of a Japanese military railway intending to link Bangkok and Moulmein (now Mawlamyline), a large seaport in Burma (now Myanmar), through 350 miles of dense jungle by way of the Three Pagodas Pass, which linked Thailand and Burma. Of course, this was not known at the time of the transportation.

The 258-mile stretch of the railway between Ban Pong and Thanbyuzayat was known as the Railway of Death.

According to the Japanese, Ban Pong was a wonderful camp with its hospital completely equipped. However, Cary Owtram, now Colonel of the 137, who arrived later than BB in Ban Pong due to illness, was of the opinion that, "in England, the RSPCA would have brought proceedings against anyone keeping cattle in such a place!"

Lieutenant Colonel Charles Cappe of the Australian Infantry Brigade thought the conditions at Ban Pong were deplorable.

The Japanese guards, having their first experience of directly controlling prisoners, became "well-nigh hysterical" in their efforts to deal with the simplest situation. Orders were conflicting, tempers were lost, and many prisoners, both officers and men, were struck without reason.

Each barrack commander was given an initiation booklet entitled, 'Instructions for Passing (i.e. casual labour) Coolies and Prisoners of War', which set out in the clearest terms the do's and don'ts of behaviour within the camps, and the consequences for any breaches of that behaviour.

No transport from Ban Pong Station was provided for the carriage of heavy personal gear and stores to the camp, so everything had to be manhandled by men already completely exhausted from lack of proper food and sleep.

In the camp, the huts were built of bamboo, with palm leaf roofs. They were 50 yards long and 20 feet wide. At the end of each hut, there were the latrines, which were nothing more than shallow trenches with palm tree coverings and from which the stench was indescribable.

Two hundred prisoners were allocated to each hut. Officers and other ranks were kept apart. On raised platforms, each man was allocated three feet of space in which to sleep, dress and keep all his worldly possessions. There was no water actually in the camp. There was, however, a well near some cookhouses some 200 yards away from the main camp, from which each POW was allowed one bucketful per day.

In his memoirs, 'A 1000 Days on the River Kwai', Colonel Cary Owtram sets out the camp's daily routine:

07:30 Rise and Roll Call.

08:00 Shave, wash etc. all in one and a half pints of water

09:00 Breakfast, rice and vegetable stew

13:30 Lunch, rice and vegetable stew

16:00 Tea, without milk, in a dixie

18:30 Supper, rice and vegetable stew (minus meat)

21:00. Roll Call

22:00 Lights Out

It seems that the meat content of the stew diminished with every meal.

However, these were relatively easy days before the heavy, heartbreaking, backbreaking manual work of railway construction began. Indeed, most camps were unguarded, there being no obvious places to which to escape.

Each day, the majority of the POWs in Ban Pong, (apart from one or two necessarily left in camp such as cooks etc.) were marched about three miles up-country to a place called Nong Pladuk, where they were employed to build another camp, the first contingent arriving there on 20th June 1942. They were tasked with clearing the forests and building barracks and workshops.

Nong Pladuk was destined to be the starting point or base camp for the notorious Thai-Burma railway, and with the other camps in that stretch was to be BB's 'home' from 20th June 1942 to 3rd October 1942, when he was moved to Tarsau where he spent about two years before he was moved again on 15th July 1944 to Tamuang (Camp 39K). There he spent another six months up to 28th January 1945. He was then moved again to Kanchanaburi, where he was imprisoned until 26th July 1945. Finally, he was moved to Nakhon Nayok, which is where he was on 14th August 1945 when the Japanese surrendered and agreed to lay down their arms.

At this stage of the war, there were three types of POW camps: branch camps, in which most of the POWs were imprisoned, and which were operated and controlled by the Imperial Japanese Army; detached (smaller branch camps); and dispatched (transit) camps. There were even smaller camps located in or close to factories or mines which were operated and controlled by the companies running the particular factories or mines. Famous names responsible for the camps and benefiting from slave labour included Hitachi, Kawasaki, Mitsubishi and Matsui. Many of these companies were the subjects of legal actions by ex-POWs after the war. None of the camps were subject to a national regime, the control and operation of each of them being solely in the hands of each camp commandant, and so the experiences of POWs varied widely from camp to camp, dependent on the personality and whim of each camp commandant.

Every morning, orders would be given to the senior officers who, in turn, relayed those orders to the NCOs and others. The orders usually concerned the work to be done that day. On one occasion, all officers were ordered to relinquish their badges of rank and display only one pip on the left breast pocket.

On another occasion, it was ordered that all Japanese army guards had to be saluted, regardless of their rank.

The barracks within the camp at Nong Pladuk contained between 200 and 300 prisoners. The camp was originally intended to hold

2,000, but it gradually expanded to hold 8,000.

Thai-Burma Railway

Actual construction of the railway line started on 16th September 1942. On the same date, construction started at the other end of the line.

As the railway progressed, Nong Pladuk was mainly used as a transit camp from where the POWs were transported or forced to march to more distant camps along the route of the railway. These camps were numbered according to the distance in kilometres from Nong Pladuk, and it is clear from the map how many camps were actually constructed. For example, Tamuang was Camp 39.

Approximately 23,000 British prisoners, 12,000 Dutch, 5,000 Australian and 7,500 other nationalities passed through Nong Pladuk.

In December 1943, a second camp was built nearby. However, later in the war, due to the camps' close proximity to the railway lines, both camps were inadvertently attacked by Allied bombers, resulting in about 100 POW deaths.

The liaison officer in charge of Ban Pong whilst the POWs were in transit to and from Nong Pladuk was Battery Captain Jerry Coombes, whose last battery position had been on the beach at Singapore as commander of the survivors of the 350 Battery of the 137.

John Harold Henry (Jerry to everyone) Coombes was an amazingly charismatic character.

Born in 1906 in Guernsey, his mother died when he was 12. He attended Elizabeth College in Guernsey from where he won a scholarship in mathematics to Pembroke College, Oxford University.

As there was conscription in force in Guernsey, he was commissioned in the Royal Guernsey Light Infantry as a second lieutenant, even though he was in full-time education, undertaking his military service during university vacations.

In 1928, after a bout of double pneumonia which caused him to miss his Oxford degree examinations, he took a job in the Sudan as an inspector of cotton plantations and where he learned to speak and write Arabic.

He remained in the Sudan for four years, and then returned to Oxford to continue his studies and to take up a part-time teaching post.

In 1939, he finally gained his MA degree from Oxford, just in time to be called up.

He was sent with the BEF to France as a captain in the Royal

Artillery, although shortly afterwards he transferred to the RAF. He was captured at Dunkirk, but managed to escape and remained with the RAF until 1941, when he was transferred back to the Royal Artillery and posted to command the 350 battery of the 137, meeting BB for the first time. He sailed with the regiment to Malaya, and took part in the battle of Jitra and the subsequent actions in the retreat. He was eventually captured at the same time as BB after fighting a rearguard action on the beach of Singapore.

In his memoirs, entitled 'The Ban Pong Express', he recorded memories of his time as a POW at Nong Pladuk. He participated in "the stand" (see Chapter 15) in that camp and survived various other camps and hardships until the Japanese surrender in 1945. He was mentioned in dispatches in 1946, in recognition of his conduct in the Malayan campaign.

He eventually returned to the UK in 1947, seeking to join the Royal Artillery in the regular army, although turned down as he was considered too old.

He then joined the Royal Army Education Corps as a captain. In 1949, he was appointed a lieutenant colonel. In 1951, he was further promoted to the rank of full colonel and chief education officer, Anti-Aircraft Command.

He had a long career in army education, returning to Singapore in 1954 as chief education officer Far East.

He produced several English newspapers in Korean, Malayan and Gurkhali whilst based in Malaya and Hong Kong. He also established British, Gurkhali and Malayan children's schools. His life, which, after the traumas of the POW camp seemed perfect, was to change in an instant. Whilst driving a car in Singapore, he accidentally killed a pedestrian. In the subsequent court proceedings he was found guilty of negligent driving and was sentenced to six months' confinement in Changi jail, the same place where he had been held for a time as a POW.

His life had gone full circle.

The collision ended his army education career, and he resigned his commission and returned to the UK.

However, his life was to take another turn when he replied to an advertisement placed by the Pakistan Government for the position of principal of the Cadet College Mirphur Khan. He was given the post and started work on the 20th March 1958.

Needless to say he made a great success of the position. He was regarded as the real father of the unit. Through his hard work, it became an outstandingly successful institution, moving, in 1959, to a new campus in Petaro, near Hyderabad.

He remained in this position until he retired in 1965.

Following the death of his first wife Alice, he remarried in 1974. With his new wife, Elsie, he returned to the cadet college at Petaro for one last reunion and grand reception.

At the college, he was considered to be a legend and a great hero in the cause of education in Pakistan.

After retirement from Petaro, he became a deputy director of education for the Anglican diocese of Southwark between 1968 and 1974, when he finally retired to his house at Sellindge in Kent.

In 1978, he suffered a stroke, and was well cared for by Elsie until his death in that same year.

Certainly, a life well lived.

However, all that was ahead of him. In Ban Pong POW camp, Jerry, using all his charms, had managed to persuade the Japanese to let him go into the local village to purchase necessary food for the camp, where he would chat to all and sundry. The Japanese were not happy about all the gossip and they decided that they would appoint a new liaison officer to replace him.

BB said, talking about Jerry Coombes, "so they, the Japanese, had him thrown out and they had to appoint a new liaison officer. As I was Orderly Officer for the day, I became Liaison Officer as well, purely by chance."

By late June 1942, most of the POWs (including BB and many men from the Blackpool Regiment) had been moved from Ban Pong to Nong Pladuk, where BB remained as Liaison Officer.

14. BB'S INVOLVEMENT WITH BOON PONG

Most of the books by and about the POWs and their personal memoirs, refer to Boon Pong as he was well known to everybody on the POW side. How the details of his operation were kept from the Japanese will never be known. Perhaps he bribed some of them to keep quiet. However, BB was in fact one of the few POWs who had full knowledge of what Boon Pong was doing, and actually met him face-to-face several times with that knowledge.

Boon Pong was a merchant in Kanchanaburi and sympathetic to the Allied cause.

BB recollects how his meetings with Boon Pong came about: "In June 1942, before leaving for Ban Pong, we had an in-camp lecture by a former chief of police, I think, who told us that when we arrived at our destination, which could be somewhere in the north of Malaya, we might be contacted by agents of the Chinese underground, the KMT. KMT was the abbreviation for the Kuomintang, or Chinese Nationalist Party. In order to make sure that any contact was genuine, a person so contacted should write on a piece of paper or on the ground the letters KMT and if the contact was genuine, he or she would alter the letters to RMP. At the time, I do not think any of us were too impressed by this type of 'John Buchan' action and paid no attention to it, except to put it in the back of our minds. We eventually arrived at Ban Pong and after a short time moved to Nong Pladuk and built the camp there. I happened to be the Orderly Officer of the day for the regiment when Jerry

Coombes, who was doing liaison, fell foul of the Japanese and was dismissed. I was appointed by the Japanese because I was on the spot when Jerry was ousted. From then on, the little fellows always shouted for "Briggsu" when they wanted something. This proved beneficial in the long run as I was able to persuade them that the canteen should be replenished every week, and they detailed two Korean guards to accompany me into Ban Pong each Tuesday for that purpose.

On the first visit, they had received specific instructions where they had to take me and we arrived at the branch of the Japanese firm Kobe Marine Co., which was a large type of warehouse on the banks of the river. The usual courtesies and refreshments were exchanged, i.e. iced coffee, cigarettes, bananas etc., and after about 30 minutes we got down to dealing.

At this time, I was aware that a Chinaman who spoke good English had joined the conversation. He was able to help the guards, myself and the shopkeepers. He was a big man and seemed to have a certain amount of authority in his voice. We then visited the Mitsubishi Trading Co. and eventually we arrived at a sort of stationer's shop, where the guards became involved with two rather attractive Chinese girls. Whilst the usual chat was going on, I was surprised to be asked by the Chinaman whether I was from Nong Pladuk Camp. Who was I? What was I doing in Ban Pong? How many people were in the camp? And many more questions. It was at this moment that the lecture came back to me and I wrote on a paper KMT and he immediately made the correction to RMP. To say I was surprised was an understatement.

The Chinaman knew all about the camp at Chungkai, where the regiment's Colonel Owtram was then in command owing to the Japs not allowing him to join his fellow members of the 137 in Ban Pong camp. The Chinaman said that he would be in Ban Pong every Tuesday and not to look for him, but that he would find me. That was how matters carried on and every week I went into Ban Pong and we met and exchanged information. Among other news items he informed me about the V Organisation operating from Bangkok and from time-to-time letters were received from them via the trains which stopped at Nong Pladuk station. The letters were handed to a sergeant major but they were addressed to me 'Lieutenant A. Burt Briggs' and always signed V.

He told me about the next planned move up-country of a party of 150 men to build the new camps for the railway battalions coming up in October, and also that I was to lead the party and be in charge. I must admit my admiration for his knowledge went up when about two weeks later Major Chida, the Camp Commandant at Nong Pladuk and later to be tried for war crimes, called "Briggsu" in and asked me to select a party of 150 men to build huts for the Japanese and named several people who had to be in the party. He wanted so many tailors, so many joiners, so many this, so many that, and he wanted 149. I said, "that's a funny number. Why 149?" "I have not decided who is to go in charge yet," he replied.

When it was completed, I gave the list to Major Chida and he put my name at the top and said that I was to be in charge. So, I went up in charge of this party of 150 men, with five other officers and myself. I was only a humble lieutenant, but it did not make any difference as I had been put in charge of the party. We all wore one star, so nobody knew what rank we were really.

The whole journey up-river by barge took us about four or five days, some 106 miles in all. We left a small party of 20 and one officer at Wampo. A small party including myself and four other officers got off at Tarsau. We sent another 20 men up to Tonchan, another 20 men up to Konyu and another 20 men to Kinkaseki. That group of camps became known as Four Group, and was administered from Tarsau. In October, several parties, each of 600 men, came up from Singapore to the various camps. But they did not come up by barge – they were made to march up from Ban Pong, up the line of the jungle road to whichever camp they were going to, and eventually they were distributed in the camps right up to the Three Pagodas Pass.

Wampo was one of the worst camps. When the first POWs arrived, there were no hospitals, no cookhouses and no accommodation, though some of these facilities were provided in a limited way for the Japanese Railway Board and the Korean guards.

Consequently, the POWs had to sleep and eat out in the open jungle, which had to be cleared. Huts, latrines and a hospital then had to be erected by the POWs, who were mainly ill and malnourished. The food consisted of hot ground rice and tea for breakfast. Lunch was boiled rice, tea and salt. Supper consisted of boiled rice and a thin watery vegetable stew made with marrows.

It took two weeks' hard work to construct the basic accommodation, but then the even harder work on the railways had to begin.

Kinkaseki was one of the largest camps, and near the outer limits of the camps controlled by Group Four. The thousands of POWs in that camp had to clear the jungle of all big trees to make space for the railway line to be constructed. It was incredibly hard work in the stifling heat, and on meagre rations consisting mainly of rice.

This camp had a very high death rate. The camp hospital was just another miserable hut where many fine young men died in squalor. The Japanese did not care. Their one aim was the completion of the railway. If a prisoner was not working, he was dying and so what? There were plenty of prisoners available.

Surrounding the camp was an ever expanding area of graveyards.

Konyu, some 90 miles north of Nong Pladuk, ultimately consisted of four camps, but in the early days of the railway construction there were only two camps, named Konyu One River Camp and Konyu Two Camp.

The occupants of the Konyu camps were committed to work on Hellfire Pass, a massive rockface sitting squarely on the route of the intended railway and through which a passage had to be cut. This was accomplished by drilling holes in the rock and inserting explosives and blasting. The prisoners then followed up to clear all the rock and debris in preparation for the next blasting. With their bare hands, they would collect everything into baskets, to be dumped then to one side.

They had no shoes. They would work in intense heat, and in a severe white rock glare, with nothing to protect their eyes, under the control of guards forcing them to work ever harder with shouts of "speedo" and hitting them whenever they felt like it. Exhausted after a day's work, the men had to stagger back in the darkness to minimal food, drink and medical attention.

On this terrible part of the railway, 69 men were beaten to death by the Japanese guards in the 12 long weeks it took to build the cutting, with many more dying from cholera, dysentery, starvation, and exhaustion.

BB's story continues.

"Anyway, the usual Tuesday visit to Ban Pong took place, and I was informed that I would be contacted at Tarsau somewhere up-country or possibly in Kanchanaburi, and that the rest of the 137 captured up-country after the Slim River defeat on Jan 8th 1942 was being brought to Nong Pladuk. Finally, in July or August 1942, a Chinese named Boon Pong made contact with me when I was taken by the Korean guards to purchase some canteen supplies at his shop, and he informed me that we should meet again. After that, we met on each of his trips up river to Tarsau and other places. He was the messenger between all camps and the V Organisation in Bangkok. Lieutenant Colonel Knights, Camp Commander at Tarsau after all the battalions had come up from Singapore in October-November 1942, carried on the liaison with Boon Pong – both at Tarsau and Tamuang. Many times he went through the fence himself to collect drugs and cash for the inmates of the various prison camps."

Lieutenant Colonel A.E. Knights DSO MC MM TD, the CO of the 4th Battalion, Royal Norfolk Regiment, was captured at the surrender of Singapore. He was imprisoned in the Sime Road Camp until October 1942. He was then transported to Tarsau where he became Camp Commander of the Allied POWs. He remained in Tarsau up to May 1944. He was then moved to Tamuang and then to the officers' camp at Kanchanaburi. Finally, in June 1945, he was moved to Nakhon Nayok, from where he was liberated in 1945.

BB resumed: "After the war, when we started the reunions at Blackpool, I had obtained more information about the 'V' setup and so I wrote to the Borneo Company Limited and asked them to confirm that their company was the one that had transferred their assets in Thailand to the Swiss Consul and that these sums of money were used for the benefit of the POW camps. They confirmed and gave me the names of a Mr. Heath and another gentleman and lady who had been employed by them and we invited them to the reunion. I never did find out if they were reimbursed for their splendid actions during the period 1942-45. I kept in touch with Boon Pong and saw him when I visited Bangkok after the war. His granddaughter wrote to me when he died.

The V Operation was controlled from the prison camp in Bangkok where all the civilian internees were held. As it was a Thai gaol the inmates had no trouble in obtaining all their requirements and sending help to us. I believe also that a French lady was very prominent in the organisation."

The story of Boon Pong is expanded and confirmed by Colonel Cary Owtram in his book. Boon Pong managed to communicate with Colonel Owtram whilst he (Owtram) was CO of Chungkai POW camp and told him that he could have medical supplies if Owtram would write a letter undertaking to approach the British Government after the war for reimbursement of any outlay. When you think about it, this was an astonishing show of confidence, as in 1942 the outcome of the war was very much in the balance. Owtram wrote the necessary letter and eventually 10,000 Thai dollars were smuggled to Owtram. He was able to use them for the benefit of the camp and especially the hospital.

In addition to his general store, Boon Pong also had an interest in a motor haulage business and in several other commercial enterprises. He persuaded the Japanese to allow him to deliver supplies to the POW camps at Chungkai, Ban Pong, Nong Pladuk and Tarsau. He usually delivered supplies in person in his motorboat or he sent his wife or daughter with them. On one occasion at Tarsau, his wife swam across the river with urgent medical supplies as no boat was available.

When the Japanese finally surrendered, he immediately supplied thousands of pounds worth of goods on credit and also advanced thousands of pounds of British currency simply on the promise of repayment.

Every care was taken by those to ensure that he was repaid in full and, in due course, he was awarded the King's Medal for the courage he displayed in the war. Unfortunately, after the war he was attacked and shot by the Thai police in mistaken retribution for his collaboration.

In 1947, he fell into financial difficulties and so a collection was organised for him, with which he was able to start the Ban Pong Bus Company, and which continued to be operated by his sons after his death. For his services, he was given the George Cross and was awarded an MBE by the British Government in 1948.

BB kept in touch with Boon Pong until Boon Pong's death in 1982, when he received the following from Boon Pong's granddaughter:

"With my deepest sympathy to announce Mr. Boon Pong's sudden death on January 29th 1982

Sincerely yours,

Mrs. Amornsri Submoke

Boon Pong's granddaughter

"I cannot say, and I will not say

That he is dead, he is just away!

With a cheery smile, and a wave of the hand

He has wandered into an unknown land,

And left us dreaming how very fair

It needs must be, since he lingers there,

And you, O you, who the

Wildest yearn

For the old-time step and the

Glad return,

Think of him faring on, as dear

In the love of There, as the love of Here;

Think of him still as the same, I say,

He is not dead – he is just away!"

(From James Whitcomb Riley)

BB replied immediately.

February 15th 1982

Dear Amornsri,

Your sad letter arrived today on the anniversary of the fall of Singapore and I was much sorrowed at the news of your Grandfather's sudden death. I had the honour to know him for nearly 40 years and every Christmas when we sent each other greetings I was always reminded that if he had not helped us the way he did under great danger a great many Prisoners of War would not have come home to England. He was always cheerful and he did the impossible for many camps and we shall always remember his smiling face and gentle ways.

The visits to his emporium in Kanchanaburi for coffee and a smoke and a general talk about the help he gave us during the years 1942 to 1945 will always be treasured in my remembrances.

I would appreciate a small photograph of his smiling face if is at all possible in order that my grandchildren can see the good Samaritan who was able to help me in my need during the dark days we worked on the Railway of Death.

Yours very sincerely and with deepest sympathy to all the

members of your family. HE WAS A GREAT MAN.

BB

Boon Pong had been so well known in Thailand that a Thai Television soap opera was made about his life, and he was featured in a documentary film, 'The Quiet Lions', which related to the war experiences of himself and the Australian hero 'Weary' Dunlop.

15. THE STAND AT NONG PLADUK
SEPTEMBER 1942

In addition to his dealing with Boon Pong, BB features prominently in the famous stand at Nong Pladuk POW camp and relates the story as follows:

"In early September 1942, an event that is without parallel in the long history of the 'Railway of Death' took place at Nong Pladuk in Thailand. I had moved with the first two battalions which had been sent up to Ban Pong in June 1942 to a small village called Nong Pladuk, further east, to build a camp at the site of the start of the ill-fated railway. After various reports that the engineer company in charge of our part of the line had inflicted several considerable beatings, Major Paddy Sykes went out on a working party to investigate. He arrived just in time to see Sergeant Bhumgara RA struck on the head with a large bamboo pole and knocked unconscious. The victim was then taken back to the camp and the matter was reported to the Japanese CO, who was informed that unless these beatings ceased the POWs would not go out to work the next day. The British COs, Major Eddie Gill of the 137 and Major Paddy Sykes, also demanded an apology from the Japanese and the removal of the offending Japanese from all working parties.

The following day, as no satisfactory assurance had been received from the Japanese, the two COs refused to order the trumpet to be blown for the morning parade, so the Japanese blew it instead. The men assembled and were counted. They were then ordered, "left turn, quick march", and nobody moved, so the interpreter was brought out and we told him that because of the beating of people on the railway by the Japanese we were not going to suffer this ill-treatment as it was quite against the Geneva Convention. The Japanese thought that was very funny, as they had never heard of the Geneva Convention. However, we said that we would not go out until we received a promise that they would stop this beating-up of soldiers. So they lined us up, all two yards apart, and gave the order again. Nobody moved. The guards for the working parties were left standing looking on whilst Major Chida and Lieutenant Tanaka harangued Major Gill and Major Sykes.

After a short time, all prisoners were ordered on parade as the Japs did not believe that the troops were behind the officers. The camp fell in and again Major Chida ordered the COs to take their men out to work. Both refused unless the Japanese would give satisfaction over the beating-up of the day before. The Japanese would not agree and Japanese guards then marched the two COs off to the guard hut, followed by Major Chida, who by this time was in full dress uniform complete with sword. Evidently, he had thought that stronger measures were required and had grabbed a rifle from one of the guards and tried to load it. The guards, who were Korean, were armed with British rifles captured in Singapore, but Major Chida, with no knowledge of the workings of the rifle, was unable to load a round and threw the rifle away in disgust. God knows what would have happened had he succeeded in loading it.

Whilst this was going on, the interpreter, an elderly Japanese named Ishikura, addressed the various section commanders in the same manner but received the same response. He had a quavering voice and his screech of, "you must engage in outside work, I order you to engage in outside work", was met by the same reply from each section commander – "I will engage in outside work only when my colonel orders me to do so."

By this time a platoon of some 60 Japanese soldiers had arrived from the Japanese POW HQ in Ban Pong. They were in full fighting kit and armed with machine guns, which they positioned giving them enfilading fire on to two ranks of officers. They were ordered to load and again the officers were ordered to give the command to go out to work, but the same response was made. By this time, Lieutenant Tanaka was livid and he proceeded to pull out an odd man or two from the ranks and, waving his sword at each of them, gave each of them the order to go out to work. All signified that they took the same attitude as their commanding officers so the Japanese ordered the guards to aim at the officers with their loaded rifles and repeated the order. It was to no avail; all stood firm. The Japanese then tried a new ploy. They spoke to each individual with the suggestion that the officers were to be taken away and that the men would be better treated in the future. They also contrived to split the resolve of the two battalions by inferring that it was only the 11th Division battalion that had been troubled with this awkward Japanese guard and not the 18th Division battalion. This persuasive talk had some effect, as some men did go back to work.

One Anglo-Japanese who, when asked by the Japanese why he was refusing to take orders from them. "Why do you stand with these English? You are coloured like us." He replied, "I may be bloody well coloured, but I'm a British subject, see?"

It was now about 11:30am and all the POWs who were left were lined up in three ranks, two yards apart and two yards between each man, facing the sun. The officers were lined up 100 yards in front and all were stood to attention. The greater majority were in their usual attire, naked apart from a pair of shorts, very brief, or a fundoshi, a type of jock strap, Japanese style. Japanese guards strolled up and down the ranks and any relaxation from their fixed stances was punished with jabs from the bayonet or a clout from the rifle butt, helped along with the usual Japanese expletives which sounded like, "kora! Baka yaro!" and which roughly translated means, 'you there! Stupid fellow!' The guards were changed every 20 minutes, but permission for the men to go to the latrines was refused. Men with diarrhoea had to excrete where they stood, in the ranks, until conditions became too foul even for the Japanese and little pits were dug in the immediate rear. The hours passed with the only relief being surreptitious movement from one foot to the other, when a guard had just gone past. The working party returned for their lunch and were made to eat in front of the parade, which they did with embarrassment and in complete silence. The heat in the afternoon was terrific, well over 100 degrees, and several men fainted, but the Japanese only allowed the casualties to be carried to the trees and, when recovered, returned to their place in the parade. The scorching sun was, by this time, beginning to burn and one or two were removed to the hospital.

Five officers were not on parade. Captain Ewart Escritt (Major Sykes' second in command) was on an abortive six-week language class outside the camp, having been specifically asked by Major Sykes to attend. I, as Canteen and Liaison Officer, had gone to Ban Pong for supplies but had been kept informed of events by the ration truck driver as I went to and from the camp with supplies. In addition to Captain Escritt and myself, Captain Christopher Ross, the Padre; Captain 'Fruity' Moisson, the Messing Officer; and the Quarter Master Captain Fred Hayes were not on parade.

When I returned from Ban Pong I was met by the Japanese officer, Major Tanaka, with the demand, "where have you been, the soldiers will not work?"

Major Tanaka was reminded that Tuesday was canteen day and that the liaison officer appointed always went into Ban Pong with the ration lorry on a Tuesday. We had always insisted that this day was the best for all concerned. Little did the Japanese know that every Tuesday the Liaison Officer (usually myself) was met by a representative of the V Organisation from Bangkok, who imparted news and received a full account of what was happening in the POW camps.

Although remonstrations were made by Captain Escritt and myself to Major Chida and Major Tanaka every half hour, no impression was made on the Japanese until they requested the appearance of the other three officers for discussion. The Padre, a tall man compared with the Japanese and who wore a Gurkha hat, together with the Messing Officer, Captain Moisson, and the Camp Quarter Master, Captain Fred Hayes, joined the two negotiators, Captain Escritt and myself, in the Japanese office and were all paraded round the Japanese officer's desk and through the interpreter were asked, "do you obey the orders of Major Chida or

Colonel Gill?"

The first person asked was Captain Ewart Escritt, who replied, "I obey the orders of Major Chida given through Colonel Gill providing they are within the best humanitarian principles".

This was accepted with some satisfaction by the Japanese. All the officers made the same reply and thanked heaven that Ewart was in the firing line first, with such a ready and convincing statement. The only change in the replies came when the question was put to the Padre and as the Japanese were sitting down and the Padre was standing at the bottom of the table, they were looking skyward when they requested his reply, which was, "I do not take my orders from Major Chida or from Colonel Gill, but from above".

He finished his answer with a pointed finger to the heavens. This brought consternation to the face of the interpreter who had difficulty in putting the Padre's words into Japanese including the pointed finger. Both Major Chida and Major Tanaka looked upward for guidance and with the usual Japanese expression of "nanda" requested, "who is above?" The Padre, looking very pained at their ignorance, replied, "it is the Senior Chaplain who is above." Again, he pointed to the roof of the hut. There was more upward searching by the Japanese round the table for this person, but to no avail until Major Tanaka with a big smile on his face said, "I know, you mean Charlie Chaplin."

The smile, however, soon vanished as the Padre, pointing upwards again, said, "you know, up above. It is the Lord Jesus up above who gives me orders." This was relayed to the Japanese, who decided that they had heard enough, and through the interpreter said, "oh yes, yes, yes, right. All then go."

This statement brought the meeting to a close and I, together with Major Tanaka, appeared in front of the men and informed them that agreement had been reached as to further treatment on the working parties outside and if they answered 'yes' to questions put to them through the Liaison Officer they would be permitted to return to their huts, and all would be well. Moving over to the officers, the same speech was made but unfortunately one officer was not there.

He had slipped out of line in the dark and ventured into the huts for a drink and his vacant place was noticed, so the officers had to wait a further three hours before they were allowed to call it a day. This was after listening to the translation of Major Tanaka's speech by Ishikura:

"Major Tanaka had resolved to punish all soldiers severely for disobedience to Japan's rule and was very 'dishonoured' at their conduct, but 'Honest Briggs' had convinced him of a misunderstanding and that they would really obey Japanese commands if given through their Colonel. He had given full apology for the beating-up and assurance that it would not happen again. Would we honourably assure him such occurrence would not be repeated?"

"All answered 'Yes'. The guards were withdrawn and everybody moved away but not before Major Tanaka called them back and said, 'I give present to you', and he handed to the officers a pressure lamp which had been carried by the interpreter. A result of the gift was that the Japanese were left in the dark.

Nobody was hurt physically, but the Japanese lost a great deal of face and next day an officer from the HQ of the Japanese authority named Lieutenant Ketsu Fujii, (the troops nicknamed him 'Edward G' because of his similarity both in his looks and his gangster actions) made a point of seeking out this 'Honest Briggs'. He informed me that I was 'a clever talker' and that when the opportunity arrived he would kill me for bringing dishonour on Japan's face. He spoke reasonable English and was a stranger in the camp, but his use of the word 'kill' as though it had about three 'e's in it was, to say the least, a little uncomfortable.

I didn't see him again for about two months and then I met him on the railway, up-country. I had left the camp for some reason, but I wore an armband which entitled me to leave whenever I wanted, provided I had a valid reason. He again uttered those terrible words, "I keel you". I met him about three times, over the next two years, and on each occasion I was greeted with, "ah Briggsu, I keel you", and he would slap his sword with expectation. But each time the conversation was, fortunately, in a crowd of people, so I survived.

The local Japanese were obviously shaken by this mass demonstration, and conditions improved. The supervisory Japanese Railway unit was moved to Penang, and the new unit waved a big stick, but not on the scale experienced up-country by the new battalions coming up from Singapore.

Major Tanaka was sent up-country to organise the camps in virgin jungle along the banks of the River Kwai and I, for my honest endeavour, was put in charge of the party of 150 men."

According to journalist David Wilson, of the Blackpool Evening Gazette, BB showed great courage and endurance in the face of the enemy. BB's final comment on the stand was, "it is no easy thing to stand up to a man with a sword in his hand and say, 'no', knowing perfectly well, that he may, in the next few minutes, chop off your head or resort to other unpleasant treatment".

It was the very highest test of moral and physical courage.

As a footnote, Major Chida Sotumatsu, partly on the evidence of Colonel Toosey, was found guilty by the post war tribunal of exposing POWs to aerial attack and was sentenced to eight years imprisonment.

16. LIFE IN THE CAMPS

So, BB had met Boon Pong and had been involved in a confrontation that could have resulted in his death, and the deaths of many others.

Throughout his time in Ban Pong, Nong Pladuk and later in Tarsau, where he spent the majority of his time, and at the other camps already mentioned, BB endured all the privations suffered by each and every POW. The only relief for him were the weekly trips into Ban Pong or elsewhere, for the purpose of purchasing rations.

Tarsau camp was surrounded by trees and in the centre of a 'road' system transporting supplies and Japanese troops north to Burma. The heavily used roads were rutted and muddy and vehicles were constantly bogged down.

The camp was at the edge of a river and was later developed into a large hospital camp with an appalling reputation. Even moderately sick POWs knew that if they went there, they would probably never leave. Prisoners tried to ensure that their names were on work party lists whether they were ill or not, simply to escape Tarsau hospital.

There were, in fact, three hospital camps at the southern end of the railway. The other two were at Kanchanaburi and Chungkai, the latter camp being under the command of the former 137 CO, Lieutenant Colonel Cary Owtram.

Both these camps were in better condition than Tarsau.

It appeared that BB's luck, so evident in the stand at Nong Pladuk, had run out.

He and his fellow POWs had been posted to a camp which had the worst reputation for lack of cleanliness, illness, cruelty and forced labour.

He was destined to survive, but at what cost?

Whilst in Tarsau, he ruminated on the part he had played in stealing radio valves when he was in Kranji. The valves were utilized in nearly all the camps to produce radios. According to BB, "there were about eight radios in Tarsau alone. All the battalions that came up-country from Singapore were marched to Tarsau, which was their second port of call, where they were counted, and then it was decided where they were to be sent.

Some were sent to Wampo, some to Tonchan, some to Konyu, some to Kinkaseki, and some even further north than that, to Quintok, Hintok and Three Pagodas Pass. Sometimes there were two battalions stationed in the camp in transit up-country and each one, of course, had a water-bottle radio (a short-wave radio inside a field ambulance water bottle), which had been supplied to them in Changi. Sometimes they got a bit blasé. I remember wandering round their camp one night and you would walk into a tent and there would be someone listening to a radio. You could walk into another tent of another battalion and somebody else would be listening to a radio, which was all a little ridiculous. If anybody had been caught there would have been hell to pay. The Japanese kept on having searches but the radios were never discovered. The radios were distributed amongst the camps and I think only one was located.

When we were moved from Kanchanaburi to Nakhon Nayok, which was the other side of Bangkok, the question was how do we get the radio there? Colonel Toosey, who, by then, was in charge at Tarsau, got hold of the officers who were looking after the radios, and the POWs who were making soap from various ingredients which had been originally for the use of the Japanese officers. He arranged for the radios to be dismantled, built into bamboo, and packed in soap in the Japanese officers' kit. They were then transported into the next camp for us by the unknowing Japanese.

On another occasion, various radio parts had been brought into Tamarkan camp, inserted into bamboo, and marked with some kind of identification. The next day the bamboo was loaded on to a lorry and the Japanese drove it back into Tarsau where it was unloaded and handed over to the people who were going to build the wireless sets. So that was how they were transported. The Japanese did it for us".

However, conditions in Tarsau improved vastly when Colonel Toosey took over.

Phillip John Denton Toosey was, for a time, the senior Allied officer in Tamarkan POW camp, the site of the building of the bridge over the River Kwai.

Born in 1904, he joined the TA in 1927. By 1934, he had risen to the rank of major.

In 1939, his regiment, the 359th (4th West Lancs) Medium Brigade RA, was mobilised and saw brief action in France, before the majority of the regiment were evacuated from Dunkirk. Back in England, he was promoted to command the 135th (Hertfordshire Yeomanry) Field Regiment RA, which was quickly shipped to the Far East. He won the DSO for heroism shown in the defence of Singapore. In that action, he was deemed to be an exceptional officer and, as such, was ordered to join the evacuation fleet, but he refused to do so in order to stay with his regiment in its subsequent captivity.

The true story of the building of the bridge over the River Kwai has been told many times, and bears little resemblance to the several sanitised fictional versions. There is no doubt that Colonel Toosey was the true hero of the whole exercise.

As Commanding Officer of the camp at Tamarkan, some three miles from Kanchanaburi, he worked ceaselessly to try and ensure that as many as possible of the 2,000 or so POWs under his care would survive.

He was beaten regularly when he complained of the prisoners' ill treatment, but he tolerated the beatings, knowing that as a skilled negotiator he could extract the best benefits from the Japanese for his men. He organised the smuggling of food and medicine, dealing directly with Boon Pong. He imposed discipline, and tried to organise the camp so that it was as clean and hygienic as possible in the circumstances. He refused to allow a separate officers' mess or separate officers' quarters. He approved and organised as much delay as was possible, without incurring the wrath and punishment usually meted out by the Japanese or Korean guards. He authorised simple but effective methods to frustrate the building of any structure. For example, termites were bred in large numbers and then released on to wooden support beams. Cement was inevitably badly mixed, becoming ineffective.

After completion of the bridge, Toosey was ordered to re-organise Tamarkan as a hospital, which he did, notwithstanding the shortages of food and medicine.

In 1943, he was transferred as Camp Commander to Nong Pladuk, where he met and became friendly with BB. A year later he was moved to Kanchanaburi, and then to Nakhon Nayok Camp, where he was being held as a hostage when the Japanese surrendered in August 1945.

On returning home, Toosey resumed command of the 359 (4th West Lancs) Medium Regiment TA, and was appointed a brigadier.

He also resumed his banking career and became President of the Far Eastern Prisoners of War Association (FEPOW).

He became a JP, and, in 1964, a High Sheriff of Lancashire. He was also awarded an Honorary LLD by Liverpool University. In 1974 he was knighted by the Queen. He died on the 22 December 1975.

A true hero amongst so many.

Although each camp was different, there were certain aspects of life common to all. A particular incident could take place in Tarsau or Ban Pong, and whilst the participants in each event would be different, the pain, disease and debilitating work would be common to all.

Certainly, the treatment of prisoners varied from camp to camp. The severity of any punishments handed out would be at the whim of the various Japanese camp commandants.

They, in turn, would be in the control of a particular railway group, itself under pressure to get its part of the railway completed.

BB was asked about punishment and said, "I have not been in the habit of talking about that for the simple reason that it has been documented so well by many other people, and when I used to talk about life out in the Far East I used to talk about the lighter side of life. In other words, the funny things we got away with. But I was beaten up twice because I would not cede to orders. On a third occasion they beat me up, when they caught me out on a story and so I was boxed about the ears, which made me a little hard of hearing for the rest of my life. As a punishment, I was sent out to work. As Liaison Officer, I said I would not go out to work outside the camp, but would work in the camp in the cookhouse with the men getting firewood for them. Luckily, I never had the experience of witnessing executions."

BB was well aware that his "punishments" were minimal compared with the torture and beatings meted out to so many others.

BB knew that it was commonplace for a Japanese officer to strike his subordinate officer or the NCO equivalent, who then passed the same treatment down the chain of command ending up with the lowliest soldier, who then took the same punishment out on the POWs under his control.

BB was full of praise for the medical people in the camps: the doctors, the surgeons, the orderlies and the nurses. How they managed with the limited implements and drugs that were available was nothing short of a miracle.

BB said, "they were quite remarkable in the things they

requested. Our engineers and tinsmiths and anybody with a hobby were soon roped in to produce distillation plants and all that kind of thing, which was just what we wanted when the cholera epidemic came and hit us. Tins, which were soldered together, were taken apart, and the solder collected and made into funnels and channels and all that kind of thing. Bamboo was used as pipes through which they produced running water in various hospitals. Altogether, the medical side was so remarkable in that so many diseases and injuries were treated successfully. Tropical ulcers for instance. They soon discovered that a bit of carbolic acid, rather warm, poured through an ulcer stopped it from spreading."

Lacking medical supplies, much treatment was improvised. Artificial legs were fashioned from bamboo. Antiseptic salve was produced by an apparatus cobbled together from bamboo, rubber tubing and sawn-off beer bottles.

Cholera was rife in all the camps. In Tarsau, 32 POWs died from the dreaded disease.

BB relates, "one of them was a member of the 137. I had paid him out at two o'clock in the afternoon – it was pay day. He was actually in charge of looking after the cattle that was on the hoof waiting to be eaten by us at some time or another. They used to give us one very skinny cow for about 4,000 people. By this time, cholera had struck the local natives who had been 'shanghaied' from Malaya and brought up to work on the railway. They were just dying like flies and there was no medical equipment for them at all. All of a sudden we had cholera in the camp and cholera, of course, is spread by mouth. It was so easy to catch it by touching leaves and other things where people had been sick. I had paid him out at two o'clock and he went out with the cattle, and he was brought in round about six o'clock at night. He was dead. He had lost weight terrifically quickly in the few hours since I had seen him. I had never seen anything like it in all my life. It was a shock to see it – the death by cholera of a fellow that you had paid out his wages at two o'clock in the afternoon, dead by six o'clock."

BB was also asked about religion in the camps.

The camps consisted of men of all faiths and religions, together with atheists and agnostics, and BB emphasised the importance given to religion in the camps. All camps had places to worship, if not actual buildings of worship as not all the camps had the space or materials for construction.

BB admitted that he was not a religious man, but from an early age he had attended church each Sunday morning.

When he was at boarding school, church was compulsory every morning in the school chapel and every Sunday he went to the local church in Bromsgrove.

To achieve some sort of inner peace, the men resorted to various methods. BB advised, "the important thing was not to be too solitary and not to dwell on the impossibility of their situation, not to think that it might never end and not to worry that they might not survive".

A tried-and-tested method was talking or communicating with, or to, someone else.

The communication took various forms: one-to-one conversations, spiritual discussions, and talks given to always-willing, participating audiences.

With regard to the talks, BB said, "I used to give talks to people. Everybody gave talks. Some on what they did in previous life. Some on what they were hoping to do in the future. Most of us thought we were going to be there at least 10 years by reason of the fact that there was such a lot of land to reclaim for the railway. I used to say to myself and others, 'my grandfather was in the Boer War and he came home, my father went right through the 1914-1918 War and he came home, so I am going to go through this war and I am going home'. Now whether that kept me going I really wouldn't know, but the thought of not going home never entered my mind. The date when it was to be always puzzled me and it was not until they dropped the atom bomb that we knew we were alright.

"Granted, I was with my own local regiment and most of the people in the regiment were known to me in civilian life, especially the officers, and I suppose that helps to keep you on an even keel. You cannot be inventing any tales of what you did, because everybody knew exactly what you did. You were in the local regiment. So, of course, one didn't romance about one's life. One romanced about one's family, which I did, having had a grandfather who had been Mayor of Blackpool twice and who had been in the theatre business. I also had one or two relatives who were on the stage, and I told stories of the theatre and the stage. Of course, if they wanted to take the mickey out of me, they did so. The knowledge which I had imparted to them about the theatre was quite interesting and quite fun at times."

As well as mental relaxation, the physical side of the POWs' existence was not neglected, but one had to take into account the weakness and illness of many of the POWs.

The organisation of games and competitions in Birdwood camp was a perfect example of how to keep men fit and healthy within the limits of their capabilities.

BB continued, "in the very early days when we were all in Changi, there were playing fields. We were in fact billeted for a time at the side of the playing fields, and it seemed to rain at six o'clock every night. So, every night the officers were standing around inside the officers' hut with nothing on, and when the rain came, as it did with a big bang, it poured down, we used to stand under the eaves of this hut and we would get our nightly bath. When we got up into the jungle, you know, on 'the Railway of Death', as it was called, we used to go and bathe in the sea or in the river, and it was quite remarkable how much it rained further up-country at Three Pagodas Pass and places like that. About six hours after the rain, the river would rise about six feet in a little under an hour. Amongst my party of men when we were going up river in June 1942, there was a very good swimmer.

At the river side at Ban Pong, everybody had thrown off their clothes because we hadn't had a wash for several days on the train and we all swam in the river. At any rate, the good swimmer got bitten on his 'John Willy' by something or other, and he came back in and the doctor sort of attended to him. Later on, he was also in the party that went up river with me, and on one of the stops up river we all went for our usual swim. The Thais wouldn't go in but one of them was fishing with a six-inch bent nail. He got a bite, and there was this lad, the good swimmer, sitting on the side watching this happening. One of the Thais jumped in and pulled out a large fish. It was about probably a yard long. Very big, bulbous-looking affair. Kind of thing you see in a cartoon more than anything else, and this Thai man opened this fish's mouth to get out the nail, and when he opened it, of course, the mouth was big enough for a head to go in. An enormous size – this fish. The swimmer sort of remembered his bother with a fish down at Ban Pong and nearly fainted on the spot to think that he might have lost all he should possess. It was a good tale, and was told for many days."

One of the main topics of conversation was food. Everyone used to fantasise about food, about particular dishes and where they would like to dine.

"People were discussing what they would eat when they got home or when they got back to Singapore. They would all go and have a meal at Raffles and so on, and this or that is what they would have. Some of the meals were quite amazing. People gave lectures on what they had done in their previous lives. We had accountants talking about finance. Solicitors talking about the law. Financial people on how to invest money. People that had been church wardens talking about the church. Some people talked about the books they had written. People who had taught at schools told some funny tales about their pupils".

BB was also proud to have met and become acquainted with Colonel Sir Edward Dunlop (1907-1993) known as 'Weary' Dunlop. His nickname was a reference to his last name, Dunlop...'tyred' as in Dunlop tyre = tired= weary!

Before the war, he had been an Australian Rugby Union international.

In 1942, he was CO of a military hospital in Bandung, Java, when he was captured by the Japanese. He was made overall CO of POW camps in Java , before being transferred to Changi, from where he was moved up to the camps on the Thai-Burma railway. His dedication to his fellow prisoners and his heroism made him a legend with the troops of all nations. According to one of his men, he was, "a lighthouse of sanity in a universe of madness and suffering".

'Weary' Dunlop did such a lot for Bill Griffiths, a member of the 137 and a friend of BB. Bill had lost both his hands and his eyes in a terrible incident and Dunlop did a very good job in helping him to come to terms with his awful injuries. BB recalls meeting Bill Griffiths sometime after the war.

He saw him sitting on a bench in St. Annes-on-Sea. BB went up to him and said, "how are you, Bill?" "Oh", he replied, "how are you, Burt?" "I'm feeling very well." He was alert enough to recognise BB from the sound of his voice, and to hold a cheery conversation. That was the attitude and mind that he had despite his terrible injuries and was symptomatic of the grit and determination displayed by nearly all POWS. It was, BB thought, the enthusiasm of Dunlop which had really saved Bill.

Both Bill Griffiths and Weary Dunlop were remarkable men in their different ways.

BB was asked whether in Tarsau, the officers, NCOs and men all worked in co-operation.

"There was some difficulty in this because the remainder of the 137 and other English regiments only had about five officers for 600 men, whereas one Indian battalion had about 100 officers for the same number. Those officers, however, were only used to dealing with Indian troops, who were mainly sepoys, and so they found it very difficult to deal with British troops. As a consequence, the Indian officers did not go out in charge of work parties very often. Eventually, however, the Japanese gave an order that all men would work and that was finally agreed with the Japanese, after negotiation. BB had done his best to persuade the Japanese that officers should not work and spoke up on several occasions. For his troubles, he was beaten about the head and discharged from any further liaison with the Japanese, and ended up on a wood-collecting party.

BB was asked about stealing in the camps. He said there was very little, but one case stuck in his mind. A prisoner used to wander through a hut at night in the dark, with his hands outstretched and anything he touched, he just stole. Although he was caught, punishment was difficult as he was, in effect, being punished merely by being imprisoned in the camp. Eventually it was decided that he would be given so many orders by the officers, not to do this, or not to do that. This was considered a suitable form of punishment, as it exhausted the guilty man. The main thing, however, is that he was punished by his fellow prisoners, as they knew what he had done and that punishment, in itself, whatever form it took was worse than anything that could be inflicted on him by the officers.

BB said that there wasn't any penalty for individual prisoners personally trying to curry favour with the Japanese guards for purely selfish reasons, rather than for the general interests of the whole camp. Everyone was, in fact, trying to do just that, perhaps to get a cigarette or a whisky or whatever, from the Japanese. Most were prepared to say or do anything within reason to get what they wanted, provided their fellow prisoners were not affected.

BB was asked about his experience with other POWs, particularly whether there were powerful animosities or great friendships among the prisoners. In response, BB recounts the story of one officer he went down country with. He said, "I went on a canteen trip to Ban Pong and the river was so low I couldn't get back. So I was about five weeks down river living in a great big hut on Kanchanaburi aerodrome with a fellow prisoner, an Australian.

We were under POW conditions, and restricted, so we just lay on our backs and did nothing all day long. We were out of camp and there was no boat to take us back. We did not know each other, as usually he was in one camp and I was in another. I had taken some old Malayan money to change. Boon Pong was going to change it for me. He had been up-river selling his eggs and this money was in my haversack. I can't remember how much it was. However, when Boon Pong eventually came to deal with the exchange, the money wasn't there. Now I didn't know whether it was the Koreans who had pinched it or anyone else, but there was nothing I could do about it. I couldn't report to the Japanese that some Thai money had been stolen. So when I got back to camp, we had a bit of an enquiry as to what had happened to it, and we concluded the Koreans had actually pinched it. That was the end of it. However, many years later I wrote a letter to a former fellow prisoner in Australia. While I was a prisoner of war, I had met a captain who actually had been a lieutenant colonel in the Australian Army, but he had reduced himself to captain so that he could stay with his men. In his battalion of 600 Australians that came up, were seven brothers from a big ranch in Queensland or somewhere like that. Whenever I wanted a particular job doing, like unloading eggs or getting stores from the Japanese, I used to get these seven lads to help. They were great big Australians with big hands. When we were counting eggs, they used to pick up five in each hand and call it three. When they were counting with the Japs, they used to put five in each hand and call it two. So, we benefitted to a great extent in the number of eggs we got from the farms that belonged to Boon Pong.

The Australian captain paid one or two compliments to me. He said that I seemed to understand what life was like out there better than a fellow he met in the camp at Kanu who was a real shark, and who had tried to do him out of this and tried to do him out of that. At the end of the letter he told me his name and it was the same fellow who had gone down river with me and who said he never knew what happened to my Malayan money! Mystery solved!"

BB was also asked if there was any evidence of homosexual friendships.

He said, "when the Dutch came up, they came with a rather lot of handsome Javanese lads, boys, and I got very friendly with a Dutch officer, Louis Van Der Heist, who was a great friend of Prince Bernhard of the Netherlands. He had been out in Java and he was in this camp with us. He came in one day and said he was very, very upset. One of his men had been attacked by an English soldier who had tried to molest him. Apparently a big horny old Scotsman in a kilt had tried to ravage him. Louis was very upset until we quietened him down. I think there were one or two instances of this nature, but nobody took any notice of them."

The number of allied POWs in the camps had been a staggering 140,000. They were from Australia, Canada, Great Britain, India, the Netherlands, New Zealand and the United States. 36,000 of them had been sent to the Japanese mainland, with 11,000 of them dying in the terrible conditions of the hell ships or as a result of friendly fire by Allied bombers. The Japanese marked their storage and military transport ships with protective Red Crosses, leaving the POW ships unmarked, as inviting targets for the unknowing US airmen.

The Japanese had not actually signed the Geneva Convention of 1929, although the Japanese Emperor had agreed to its provisions.

The Japanese also failed to recognise the Hague Conventions of 1899 and 1907.

Consequently, this meant that the prisoners' basic human rights were ignored. This wilful ignorance did not just relate to the physical punishments regularly handed out, but to all the other essentials that could have made life bearable for the POWs. Notifications of capture were routinely ignored, so that loved ones at home did not know whether their husbands, relatives or friends were alive or dead.

These were the experiences of two Blackpool Regiment men: Gunner Reginald Dunne, reported missing in February 1942, and confirmed to be a POW in November 1942, and Lance Bombardier Chuck Jackson, reported missing in February 1942, and only reported to be a POW 17 months later, in June 1943.

By September 1943, just over a year and a half after the surrender, only 65% of the next of kin of British POWs had been notified of capture.

The Japanese did not care about mail, either. All outgoing letters had to be censored, and all incoming mail had to be scoured for useful information.

Piles of unopened mail was found in the Japanese officers'

quarters in nearly all POW camps on liberation. Without doubt, there would have been many more items of mail which were just destroyed to avoid the trouble of going through them. The standard cards which the Japanese permitted to be sent out averaged only four or five per POW for the whole three-and-a-half years of captivity.

Visits to the camps by the Red Cross were discouraged by the Japanese. In most cases, access was simply refused.

In fact, only 43 camps were visited and none of those on the railway. Visits were limited to two hours in total and a Camp Commander's conversation with Red Cross visitors was limited to 30 minutes each visit.

Any Camp Commanders who complained about conditions were likely to be beaten up after the visitors' departure, and many Camp Commanders simply refused to speak to the visitors at all.

A polite request to the Japanese for the exchange of sick or wounded British POWs was ignored, but there was more success with arrangements for exchange of civilian internees, when approximately 1,800 were exchanged in Lourenço Marques in Portuguese East Africa.

In most camps, the standard work schedule was eight hours a day with one day a week off, although this was seldom allowed. Those working in dispatch camps were paid by Japanese Army Regulations. The rate of pay was one sen per day per POW, which was paid to the camp by the company employing the POWs. A private soldier received 10 sen per day, an NCO 15 sen, and officers at least 25 sen per day, dependent on their rank.

The firms employing the POWs paid the Japanese army, who, in turn, passed it to a POW officer, who then paid the POWs.

Indeed, on several occasions BB had the duty of acting as a paying officer. However, the pay was in an account book and not cash. When POWs wanted to spend actual money, they received cash from the POW paying officer and they shopped outside the camp accompanied by Japanese guards. They were not allowed to buy food. Probably, most POWs were never paid.

Medical treatment was very limited and, of course, medicines were in short supply.

In an act of extreme cruelty, whenever a POW was unable to work because of illness, his food rations were cut.

Other punishments were severe .For even the mildest breach of the rules, POWs were forced to keep running either on the spot or on a defined track, or to stand to attention for hours, or kept standing with a bucket of water on their heads, or forced to put their mouths under a flowing tap.

There were, of course, many deaths.

154

PART FOUR

HOMEWARD BOUND

17. THE BEGINNING OF THE END

Work on the part of the Thai-Burma railway between Ban Pong and Thanbyuzayat, known as the Railway of Death, started on 22nd June 1942 and finished on 19th October 1943. It was 258 miles long and cost about 104,000 deaths, or more than 400 deaths per mile.

Sixty-nine miles of this section were in Burma and the remaining 189 in Thailand.

Many of the casualties of the Railway of Death were buried or commemorated: 6,982 at Kanchanaburi, 1,379 at Chungkai and 3,626 at Thanbyuzayat.

Approximately 90,000 Asian labourers perished, along with 6,318 British POWs and 2,815 Australians.

On 17th October 1943, construction gangs from Burma, working south, met with construction gangs from Thailand. They met at a point 18 miles south of the Three Pagodas Pass.

In Japan, a public holiday was declared for 20th October 1943, which was chosen as the ceremonial opening of the line.

Following the completion of the railway, POWs were moved to hospital and relocation camps for other labouring work and general maintenance. The urgency to complete the railway had gone, but that did not diminish the cruelty and treatment meted out by the Japanese to the POWs.

To alleviate the POWs' inevitable boredom, entertainment in various forms flourished. Theatres of bamboo and attap were built along with elaborate sets. Costumes and makeup were somehow manufactured and an array of entertainment provided, although not always up to West End standards.

All the productions needed actors, singers, musicians, designers, technicians and female impersonators and were immensely popular, even entertaining the Japanese and Korean guards.

In the world outside the POW camps, the war was coming to an end, although the Japanese did not appear to be aware of this. On 8th September 1943, the Italians had surrendered. D-day had come and gone. The British and American troops were battling their way into Germany. On the eastern front, the Russians were advancing steadily.

The race to be first in Berlin was on. The Americans, island by island, and at great cost, were forcing the Japanese to withdraw.

News of the Allied victories was heard on the water-bottle radios, spreading quickly around the camps.

In the final days leading up to surrender, there had been several signs that things were about to change even more dramatically.

The bombers overhead were now American B29s. The POWs in the railway camps were not to know of the increasing raids on the Japanese mainland. Unfortunately, however, there were several raids on the railway camps which caused death by 'friendly fire'.

Colonel Toosey was in command at Nong Pladuk when a bomb load hit the railway camps instead of the nearby marshalling yards, killing more than 90 POWs and wounding more than 400.

Twelve American airmen who had been shot down perished in gaol in Hiroshima when the bomb was dropped. Those in Nagasaki POW camp, only a mile from the epicentre of the bomb, were relatively lucky to 'escape' with only eight deaths and 30 injuries. However, it will never be known what later effects the radiation had on the prisoners who survived the initial blast.

On 14th August 1945, in Thailand, BB and the men of the 137 in Nakhon Nayok were somehow among the first to learn that the war was probably over.

At Kanchanaburi, on the same date, the Korean guards told the POWs that the war was over, but were disbelieved. It was only when the ever reliable Boon Pong cycled past the camp and told the POWs, "Peace. War over. War over." Gradually, the news filtered through the camps down the line of the railway. In each one, the crowds of POWs poured from their huts, to congregate where the official announcement could be heard.

The singing of God Save the King, the Star Spangled Banner, Land of Hope and Glory and Waltzing Matilda rang out the length of the railway, together with all the usual familiar soldiers' songs.

'Oh, that the dead could hear such joy.'

Officially, the war had ended at 12 noon, Japanese Standard Time on 15th August 1945, when the Emperor Hirohito broadcast to the Japanese people.

On August 17th 1945, he gave orders to the military to lay down their arms.

Later, in a great moment of history, the formal Instrument of Surrender was signed at 09:04 on 2nd September 1945, on the deck of the battleship USS Missouri in Tokyo Bay Harbour. The signatories for Japan were Foreign Minister Mamora Shigemitsu, on behalf of the civilian government, and General Yoshijiro Umezu, on behalf of the Japanese military. General Douglas MacArthur signed on behalf of the Allies.

In England, my mother received a telephone call from her father to tell her that the Japanese war was over. As an MP, he had received the news ahead of the public announcement.

Even though I was only about six at the time, I remember my mother sitting down on hearing the news and sobbing her heart out.

Would the POWs take revenge on the guards? Did they feel some pity for them?

Colonel Philip Toosey certainly did not. At Nakhon Nayok, he was summoned by Lieutenant Takasaki (for some reason nicknamed The Frong), who was in charge of the camp whilst his superior, Lieutenant Hideji Noguchi, was temporarily absent. Lieutenant Takasaki had been the hated commandant at Tamarkan, where six British escapees from the camp were executed after having been recaptured. Takasaki offered Chinese tea to Toosey, saying, "now we are friends, we can shake hands, now the war is over." Toosey refused the tea and asked what had happened to the men executed at Tamarkan. Were they executed on Lieutenant Noguchi's instructions? Takasaki admitted that the executions had not been under Noguchi's orders, but had been his own decision. There was little that Toosey could do with that information at that time, but it was used in evidence at the subsequent war crimes trials, at which Takasaki was ordered to be executed. Toosey, having refused the tea, said he was taking over the camp, to which Takasaki had no objection.

A grand parade of 1,200 officers, including BB, then followed, where it was announced that the war was over. The National Anthem, Land of Hope and Glory and Jerusalem were sung lustily, but certainly not in tune.

Captain Noguchi, who had returned to the camp, then handed over to BB thousands of letters and Red Cross parcels which had been withheld, some from as long ago as 1942.

At the same time, Colonel Toosey demanded that he be supplied with the batteries off the Japanese trucks in order that we could listen to the report of the Armistice and the cessation of war from London. Captain Noguchi would not believe that there was a radio in the camp, because he had only just moved from Tamarkan about five days before, and he thought he was fully in control. He said he would release the batteries if he could listen to the radio. Colonel Toosey agreed, and the batteries were made available. Captain Noguchi came in and listened to the London report about the end of the war, and he went out and drew his sword and said, "I kill myself". He didn't actually, but according to BB he still he got his just desserts later on.

BB was right. For his general brutality, and in particular for his part in the treatment of Captain W.N. Drower at Kanchanaburi POW camp by keeping him in solitary confinement for 77 days, he was found guilty by the War Crimes Commission and sentenced to death by hanging.

It is worth noting the part played by Colonel Toosey in the above scenario, and reminding the reader of his bravery and audacity throughout his captivity and his overall influence over the various camps, particularly Tamarkan.

There were, of course, acts of revenge. Some guards in various camps were shot whilst officers looked the other way. Some were pushed into and drowned in the latrines. In New Guinea, Japanese soldiers lined up to surrender were shot. Lesser punishments were also handed out. A hated mine boss was force-fed horse dung. Other Japanese guards were made to walk between two rows of prisoners whilst buckets of faeces were poured over them.

There were even acts of compassion towards the Japanese. In BB's camp, Nakhon Nayok, Lieutenant Colonel Albert Coates visited the adjoining Japanese hospital camp and immediately offered his medical officers and orderlies by way of assistance. The offer was refused by the Japanese officer in charge, as he said he had no authority to accept it, notwithstanding the fact that many of his men were dying.

Although the Japanese surrendered informally on 14th August 1945, and officially on 15th August 1945, it was not until 28th August 1945 that a ceasefire took effect. Everywhere, there were pockets of resistance. Field Marshal Count Terauchi, Commander in Chief of the Japanese Southern Army, refused to surrender, as did the Commander of Singapore Island, General Itagaki, although in the end he surrendered without a fight. Sporadic killing continued. In Taiwan and Borneo, written orders were discovered to eliminate all the POWs by bombs, poisonous smoke, drowning or decapitation.

So, the task was now to get everyone home. Sick POWs were still dying at the rate of 15 per day.

At the time of the surrender, across the Far East there were 750,000 Japanese of whom 630,000 were armed troops. As far as the Allies were concerned, the main task was to make safe the 123,000 POWs under the Recovery of Allied POWs and Internees (RAPWI) programme.

Another problem arose in BB's camp, Nakhon Nayok. Six-hundred men had left in April in order to work on making a road in Mergui Province, some 375 miles away.

Of the 600 men, 200 had died and another 200 were in a pitiful state. After the Japanese surrender, those that did survive were brought back to Kanchanaburi, emaciated, barefoot and in rags.

The main impression of the men's rescuers was how badly the poor survivors smelled.

BB had been lucky again as he had not been selected for this work party.

Airdrops of food and drugs in 44-gallon drums to the camps started on August 28th. With the food came warnings not to overeat or overmedicate, but unfortunately some did, with dire consequences. In 15 days, some gained 20lbs at great cost to their health, and others, with terrible irony, died as a result of being freed.

Admiral Lord Mountbatten was made Supreme Allied Commander in South-East Asia. With his wife, Edwina, he made it his business to visit as many camps as possible.

At one camp, he could not speak for the tears in his eyes as he surveyed the pitiful, joyous, throng of prisoners.

BB's camp, Nakhon Nayok, was visited by Edwina, sitting in the rear of a jeep with the Camp Commander, Lieutenant Colonel Coates. She made such a good impression on the men who had not seen a white woman for years. One POW said, "we were visited today by Lady Mountbatten wearing a row of ribbons and no stockings".

The boys were going home.

By the end of October, 71,000 prisoners had been transported from hell to their homes in India, Australia and Britain. For some paradise was to come. For others, hell in comfortable surroundings, beckoned.

Even before starting the journey home, some POWs were overwhelmed.

An unnamed prisoner, confronted by an American nurse in a spotless white uniform, was forced into dumb silence, unable to make his mouth function. He could not speak. All he could produce were tears.

Home for the POWs was by several circuitous routes – to the US, to Australia, and for the British, eventually across the Atlantic to Southampton or Liverpool.

All POWs caught up with their mail, not always receiving good news. Wives had left husbands, or mothers and fathers had died before goodbyes could be said.

Returning POWs were asked many times what it had been like. One said, "we could not tell them. When we tried, they changed the subject and soon we learned not to try."

Amidst the tears of happiness, there were tears of frustration and wonder. A POW described life as, "passing from hell to paradise in 72 hours. We even had showers!"

Arriving at Liverpool, the returning POWs were greeted by the Lord Mayor, bands, senior officers and MPs.

Conflicting moods prevailed. One ship would be gloriously noisy and celebratory. Another would be enveloped in a melancholy sadness.

A POW said, "we had come home and we felt as if we didn't belong. The only people who understood us were ourselves" – and over the years this would become more and more true.

18. BB'S RETURN TO ENGLAND

At the time of surrender, BB along with several other 137 survivors were interned at No.4 POW camp Thailand.

Very quickly, he was moved to Bangkok Airfield and then flown to Rangoon, following the line of the railway he had helped to build. In Rangoon, he was billeted at Raffles College, which had become a temporary POW hospital.

He and his fellow POWs were washed and scrubbed and given new uniforms. Eventually, he was taken to board *MS Boissevain*, a luxury liner built for the KPM Dutch Shipping Line based in Amsterdam and launched on June 3rd 1939 from Hamburg.

The journey from Rangoon was via Colombo, the Suez Canal and Gibraltar.

In Colombo, there was an astonishing welcome when arriving in what looked like a blacked-out port. Suddenly, all the lights flashed on, rockets exploded and a huge screen displayed 'WELCOME'.

Most of the POWs were in tears.

After Gibraltar and the Bay of Biscay, the *Boissevain* passed into British waters. England was clearly visible. The first real sign of home was the crossing of the Mersey Bar, but the POWs were looking for their first sight of Blackpool Tower, a figure of hope on the distant horizon.

BB, like all the survivors, had been clearly traumatised by the whole experience, although on 30th August 1945, whilst still in Thailand, he acknowledged his good fortune when he wrote to Isobel:

"...I have been very lucky all along and have been fit the whole time...We don't expect any trouble in getting home quickly. This letter must be awful to read but the very small pencil I have doesn't help much. I shall write as soon as we are out of all this. It is a great relief to know it is all over and we shall be together again very soon."

On September 3rd he wrote again from Bangkok:

"I have no doubt that you will receive a few cables before you get this, but this is my first real letter as a free man again. I have still got all your letters and photos and this morning before we leave for Rangoon I hope to get my ring etc. back. It is such a long time since we were allowed pencils and paper that this looks such a big one I don't know if I can fill it. I do hope that by now, you know we are all ok. By gosh what a day! I hope that when we arrive home you can arrange to meet me in London and we can have a few days alone together before I go home to meet everybody... as soon as we know that date of our arrival I will cable you...I am longing to see little Josephine but I don't suppose she will be so little now. It will be the biggest day of my life when I get home to you and Josephine. It is the one thing I have been waiting for for 3½ years."

On September 5th in Rangoon, and still not having set sail, BB again acknowledges his luck and makes his thoughts about the Japanese clear:

"During the whole time I have been a POW, apart from a fortnight to jaundice I have been very fit the whole time. I have been one of the very few lucky ones, consequently, I am hoping to be one of the first home. If anybody at home wants to feel sorry for the Japs tell them that the Japs murdered about 20,000 POWs in Siam alone, what they have done elsewhere, I don't know. I have not met anybody who has met a civilised Japanese."

On September 11th from Rangoon, he told Isobel that he had new glasses:

"I have just got some new glasses which make writing much easier, my eyesight has gone weaker. But that is the only thing I have wrong with me. I have been very lucky indeed… Can you get my service dress that I left at home fixed up – you know, new buttons and badges. I shall need them I have no doubt, till I get demobbed."

On September 22nd from Colombo, BB tells Isobel:

"I am on my home journey to you and Josephine. We do not know which port we shall arrive in, but we think it will be either Liverpool or Glasgow. That being the case, I shall come straight home to No.4 as soon as I can make it. The Blackpool gang are still together, and we are all very fit."

He calmly asks Isobel to get the following from Raymond Coupe in St. Annes:

2 pairs pyjamas

2 Khaki shirts and collars (Van Hanson)

2 Khaki ties

1 cloth belt for my S.D. suit

He asks that there be no welcoming party for him:

"Whatever you do, darling, about preparing a big reception for me, I only want you and Josephine to be home when I arrive. I will go and see the others when I feel like it."

In another letter from Colombo, he again raises the subject of how he will be dressed:

"Oh, by the way, will you get me a dress hat, you know, like the one you bought me at Larkhill? I still have that old one but as it was the only hat I had, it is well worn…Size 6¾ complete with gun button and grenade. I thank you."

BB's emphasis on clothes is not surprising, as he would have spent the last three-and-a-half years in rags and a fundoshi.

In another letter, he looks forward to dancing again.

On September 28th from the *MS Boissevain* in the Red Sea, he wrote to say he expected to be home on 11th or 12th October, and he gave news of the members of the 137 on board:

"We are all very fit and there are about 80 of the 137 aboard. Some others are still in Japan, some in Singapore, but the bulk of the unit are in Thailand and are following on."

He is excited and thinks that he might be able to ring Isobel the minute he lands:

"I would love to ring you as soon as I can after we have landed. If it (the telephone) is still in, let the MO know so I can get the number through enquiries. What a thrill I hope to get if I can ring you up!"

At last, the *MS Boissevain* berthed in Liverpool, on October 13th 1945 at the Princes Landing Stage, Liverpool, from where BB and the 137 had set sail for Singapore in 1941. In his own words:

*"The arrival was greeted with groans and comic remarks from my fellow ex-POWs as my sister had dismantled her black-out curtains and had cut out in white cloth the words, **'WELCOME HOME BURT BRIGGS'** in letters two feet high. I was lifted aloft and almost thrown into the Mersey by my colleagues."*

One can only imagine BB's final homecoming.

Following his war service, he was awarded campaign medals: War Medal 1939–1945, the 1939-1945 Star Medal and Territorial Decoration with Bar.

At home, BB had time to reflect – more men of the 137 had died in the camps than in fighting. Out of 759 members of the regiment, in all 224 men had died, 70 in battle, and the remaining 154 had died at the hands of the Imperial Japanese Army on the Railway of Death.

The regiment's casualty rate was almost 30%, compared with the British Army rate in WW2 of 12.59%. To add to that dreadful toll, most of the survivors were in a terrible state of mental and physical health.

Some men came back to families who, for a time, had not expected them to return. They had been reported missing or killed, and then months later reported as POWs.

All the men had to be treated with exceptional care.

A talk was given, attended by about 500 mothers, wives and girlfriends in Blackpool Library by Professor B.G. Maegraith, MA, MB, Principal of the Liverpool School of Tropical Medicine, on 'How to Treat POWs Back from the Far East'. He clearly described the three best ways to help: 1) Diet 2) Patience 3) Tropical diseases

1)   Be careful what your man eats. The main piece of advice was, 'don't let your man overeat.'
2)   Listen to his stories or accept his unwillingness to talk. Don't bottle him up, let him talk about his horror stories, or anything he wants to.
3)   Learn to identify what tropical diseases he may be suffering from.

Maybe a quick return to civilian life did not give enough time for 'sanity to establish itself decisively'.

In the words of the author of the 'Fyldecoaster' website article, "free from captivity didn't mean free from torment and ordeal. Feelings and emotions suppressed for years were now unleashed on families ill-equipped to cope or make sense of it. Families that had been advised not to talk to their men about their experiences and not expect too much; Families that took second place to fellow POWs. Families that despite the deprivations of war at home, knew absolutely nothing of what these shadows of their former selves had experienced. Families that couldn't make sense of 'new' irrational behaviours. Behaviours that had maintained some kind of survival, sanity and normality in a captive, totally alien world. In the longer term, these men expected that, as time moved on, the rest of the world would forget what they had been through. Adding to the mix of non-communication, returnees too had been instructed to 'Guard your tongue' in an official leaflet given to them on the way home."

From my own experience as the son of a returning soldier, who had seen the horrors of Dunkirk and Belsen, I can only confirm what has been said. I deeply regret my lack of knowledge and understanding, which led to a complete breakdown in communication between my father and myself. This, in turn, led to a lifetime of animosity between us. War has so many unseen casualties, of which my relationship with my father was certainly one.

In my defence, I was only six years old when my father arrived back in England. It was only as I grew older that I totally failed to understand what he had been through. He died as he had lived, in a state of agitation, anger and remorse. He shut himself out from my life and I from his.

BB was asked how his experience of war had reshaped him as a person. He said, "I wouldn't really know. I suppose it had some effect on me, when I realised that I was able to quieten the Japanese down over some trivial exercise, or some similar incident that had been committed by soldiers under my command. I suppose it did help me to deal with people when I came home. It might have done. I don't know."

BB was asked if captivity had changed his life. He replied, "Undoubtedly. Yes there is no doubt about that because you have, after all, lived through it." At an address to a FEPOW (Far Eastern Prisoners of War) conference in Northumberland he said, "really we should look upon our life out there, that it wasn't all bad. It made us a little bit more tolerant of things than we would have been. I seem to think that one thing that it did for a lot of us. We became more tolerant."

On 15th October 1945, it was announced that the Freedom of the Borough was to be conferred on the Blackpool Regiment, the 137 Field Regiment, Royal Artillery.

Favourable consideration was also given to a suggestion that there should be a permanent memorial, in the form of a club, for Ex-servicemen and women of the war service of Blackpool men and women.

19. SANITY

BB decided to return to work as soon as possible, as did many of the returning POWs. Some of them, of course, were not fit enough to work at that time. Others would never be fit enough to work again.

BB returned to banking as a Clerk in Charge at the Whitegate Drive, Blackpool branch of Martins Bank.

In July 1946, he was sent to another branch where the Clerk in Charge had had a stroke during the lunch hour. The poor man never recovered and BB never went back to Whitegate Drive. His lunchtime appointment lasted nine years!

BB also pursued his love of rugby by re-joining Fylde Rugby Club and becoming Secretary of the 'B' XV.

Unable to shake off his military past, he joined the TA again, together with Cary Owtram, Tom Spencer, Doc Tomlinson, his brother-in-law Bill Fielding, Alan Grime and several other survivors.

In 1950, BB was asked to take over as Second in Command of another regiment in Accrington, Lancashire. He did so willingly.

In 1955, Blackpool hosted a reunion of FEPOWs at the famous Winter Gardens, where nearly 1,000 people attended.

Again, luck seemed to follow BB.

Attending the reunion were Lieutenant General Percival and Brigadier Toosey.

Brigadier Toosey was a Director of Martins Bank. When he

learned that BB was an employee, he indicated that he would do something about BB's future.

Within three days, BB was asked to report to head office for an interview. From then on, he was on the promotion ladder, being made manager in 1958.

In 1956, the FEPOW National Conference was held at the Norbreck Castle Hotel in Blackpool, BB attending as Chairman of the local FEPOW Association.

Eventually, he retired from the TA. This enabled him to devote time to the FEPOW Association Blackpool Branch.

Following the death of Lieutenant General Percival, Brigadier Toosey became National President and BB eventually became President of the North West Area FEPOW Association following his retirement from banking.

In 1975, BB and Isobel made a pilgrimage to Singapore and Thailand, where BB renewed his acquaintance with Boon Pong.

In 1983, BB wrote to the Sunday Post, a weekly newspaper published in Dundee, telling the story of Colonel Toosey and the radios in Nakhon Nayok in August 1945.

On July 18th 1985, there was a service at the Blackpool Cenotaph, followed by afternoon tea at the Clifton Hotel. Cary Owtram was present, but could not be persuaded to sing, although he spoke of his pride in being associated with the Blackpool Regiment for so long.

A month later, on 15th August, the 40th anniversary of the ending of the Second World War, there was an Act of Remembrance Service for the fallen of the Blackpool Regiment at St. John's Church, where BB gave a 'Recital of the Roll of Honour'.

On 17th August, 22 standards of the local ex-servicemen's association were paraded in the Spanish Hall of the Blackpool Winter Gardens, followed by a determined march/dance to the strains of Colonel Bogey! That must have been quite a sight, both moving and humorous at the same time.

Later in the year, there was a pilgrimage back to the Far East, including a visit to Kanchanaburi Cemetery, where the FEPOW prayer was recited.

"And we that are left grow old with the years

Remembering the heartache, the pain and the tears,

Hoping and praying that never again

Man will sink to such sorrow and shame,

The price that was paid we will always remember,

Every day, every month, not just in November."

BB had some appropriate phrases for captivity in his FEPOW correspondence. He refers to the "days of the Nippon problems" when he and his fellow prisoners had been "guests of the Japanese", reminding everyone of the bonds of friendship formed at that time.

On 11th and 12th April 1988, in one of his update letters to the FEPOW members, BB reminded them of the 1985 Memorial Service at the Parish Church of St. John the Evangelist, Blackpool. "In August 1985, many ex-members of the 137th (Army) Field Regt RA (TA) assembled at the Parish Church of Blackpool for a memorial service to those of our fellow men who were killed in action or had died as a result of their labours on the Railway of Death. I read out the list of names, which numbered over 230. I felt very honoured by the Association to be asked to read this list of hallowed beings."

Later in the year, on 15th August 1988, the Blackpool and Fylde FEPOW Association held a Dedication of Plaque and Laying-Up of Standard at Blackpool Parish Church, St. John the Evangelist, Church Street, Blackpool.

BB delivered a short address: "For the fortunate few, who survived the appalling degradation of defeat, the horrendous humiliation of hunger and the daily toll of dreary death, it was felt to be our duty to erect to those who sadly paid the ultimate price a

Memorial at which it is hoped future generations will pause and pray. You by your unstinting empathetic generosity have made this possible. *Ad multos annos*."

Then followed a list of organisations, companies and individuals who made financial contributions to the Memorial.

BB wrote to FEPOW members:

"So many of those present, predominantly ORs, asked after so many of the officers in other parts of the country that I was motivated to write to all those whose addresses I knew and request a short C.V. from them in order that I could put my findings down on paper and bring you all up to date."

On September 8th 1992, BB sent a newsletter to all members of the '40 Years On Association', referring to the three-and-a-half years when they were all, "chopping trees, building railways, repairing attap huts, clip-clopping about the jungle on the way to the benjos (WCs), taking the mickey out of the Japs and other unusual Far Eastern happenings".

In the newsletter, BB recollected how "proud" 137 Regiment had been to be chosen as the Depot Regiment at the School of Artillery Larkhill, from November 1940 to September 1941, when they were mobilised. He remembered how they were, "brought up to full strength, loaded their limbers etc. and sailed off to the Far East, to Singapore. Soon after landing in November 1941, we motored at a fast rate to Jitra and fired off the ammunition loaded on the depot regiment's parade ground at Larkhill into the paddy fields, inhabited by Japanese troops. Or so we were told!!!"

On 20th April 1994, he wrote a missive to 'All surviving members of the 40 years on Club' and shared the following information: "The next Mayor of Blackpool has plans to establish a Museum in the town and it may be that items of interest belonging to the Regiment could be put on display." He appealed to his group, "anything you have that may not stand the test of time in the south of the country could be used by us up here."

For health reasons, he did not attend the Malayan Campaign Officers Annual Reunion in 1994 and was much missed.

In 1996, he shared a recent health scare with FEPOW members and proudly recounts how he met the Queen in connection with the centenary of the Grand Theatre Blackpool, of which he was Vice President and a founder of the trust that managed the theatre.

In the same year, he attended a garden party at Buckingham Palace and entertained the Blackpool FEPOWs and their wives with lunch at The Goring Hotel. He described it as a "great day".

Although he was not responsible for pursuing the compensation for the FEPOWs at the hands of the Japanese, he did much to circulate information and update his readers on progress or lack of it. "There is still no thought of any payment from Japan. The anticipation appears to be in the minds of certain FEPOWs only (1996).

In 2000, the Government announced it would make a one-off payment of £10,000 as a debt-of-honour payment and, in 2001, BB received his payment.

In 2004, BB died in his sleep. Certainly, another life well lived.

SOME MEMBERS OF THE 137

This book is about people, not military strategy. It is about young men, thrown into war, terrified and bewildered.

In my research, and as a result of my request for information in the local newspaper, various stories and personalities emerged.

Some characters had already appeared in the main text, but I have tried to say more about them, to flesh them out as it were.

Only a very small percentage of the members of the 137 are mentioned. That, in no way, diminishes those who are not.

All the members of the 137 were heroes. Those who are mentioned, by implication, pay tribute to those who are not.

Basil Akhurst

Basil was a member of the Blackpool Regiment at the outbreak of World War Two, eventually being captured at the Fall of Singapore.

He was an accomplished cartoonist having pre-war published cartoons under the name of Akki in the Blackpool Gazette.

He also designed and published postcards of the Blackpool scene after the war.

He was an architect by trade.

He has sailed back to England on RMS Corfu, docking at Southampton on 7th October 1945. He then travelled home by train, being met at 05:25 on 9th October at Blackpool North Station by his parents, who described him as 'bright-eyed and surprisingly fit'.

He commented in the local paper that 'there were no wild scenes of rejoicing among the prisoners when news of the surrender came through. We simply bunged the Japs into a little corner out of the way'.

Lionel Bradstreet RSM

Lionel's home was in Exeter. He gave evidence to a Japanese War Crimes Tribunal regarding the appalling treatment meted out to Gunner King, an Australian, by Captain Suzuki at Lieng Khan POW camp, Saigon.

Muster Parade Poster 1940

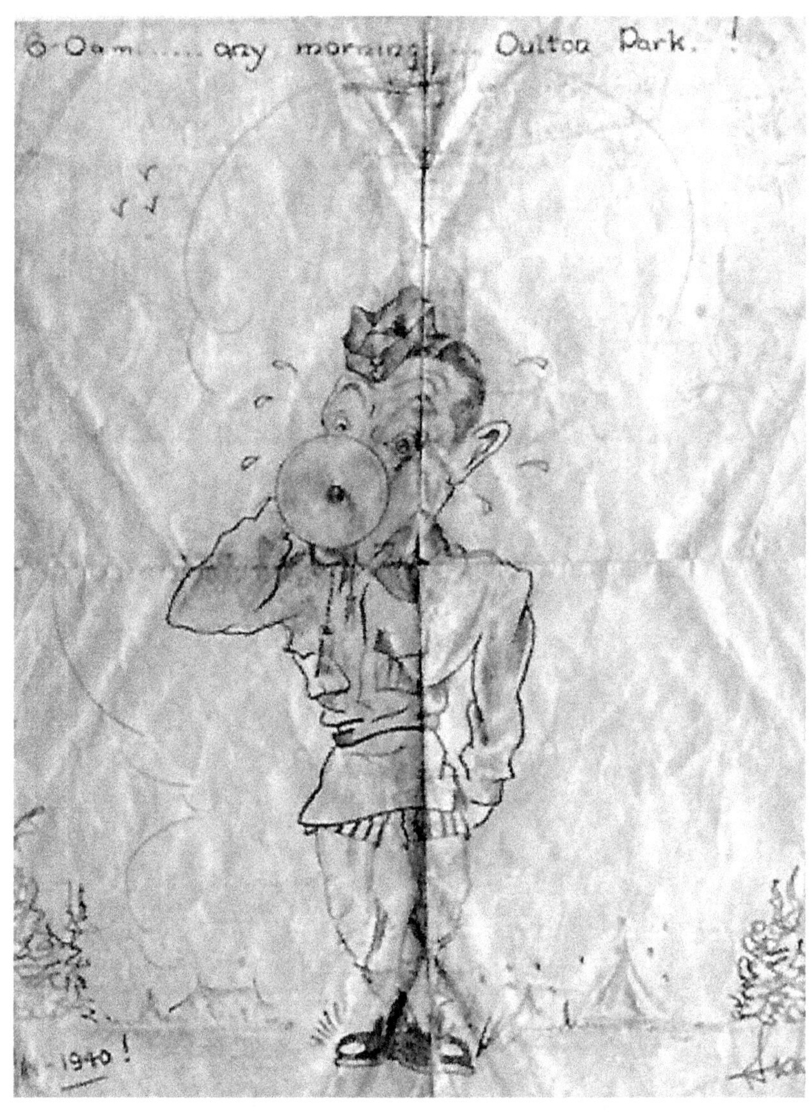

Harry Connolly Akki Cartoon

Harry Connolly

Born in 1917 in Manchester, he left home at 14 to begin a career as a professional musician, with, among others, Joe Daniels and his Hotshots, with whom he performed at the BBC.

Captured along with others at the Fall of Singapore, he arranged many concerts in the camps and was widely known as Ace Connolly and his Kings of Swing. On his release in 1945 he was shipped back to Liverpool weighing under six stone.

He married in 1946 and continued as a musician. For a time, he worked as band leader for Geraldo on the Cunard Atlantic crossings.

Retiring from music, he became a grocer and a publican, dying at the early age of 53, his death no doubt accelerated by his time in the camps.

William Edwin (Eddie) Gill - Major

He was Camp Commander of the following camps on the Railway: Ban Pong, Nong Pladuk and River Valley.

He was sent to Saigon in February 1945, and became Camp Commander of Long Thanh. He also spent a few days in Harbour Camp Saigon.

He returned to Kanchanaburi in March 1945, then marched to Nakom Nyok from where he was released on 20th August.

He gave evidence to a War Crimes Tribunal reporting the conditions at Long Thanh Camp and about Captain Suzuki, Lieutenant Hatori, and several Japanese Sergeants.

After the war he resumed his career as a solicitor.

He was much loved and highly respected in Blackpool and I am proud to say he was a family friend of my parents' generation.

On his return he told the local newspaper that the Regiment had faced its trials bravely. 'Tell Blackpool that the 137th has been absolutely magnificent throughout. Its performance in action and its endurance of privation have been excellent.'

Alan Grime - Captain

Alan was a member of the well-known and influential Grime family, who owned and managed the Blackpool Gazette Newspaper group. He was the son of Herbert Grime, Sir Harold Grime's brother. He worked in the Gazette Accounts Department and was only 20 when he joined the 137. He is mentioned in several books about the Railway. When he returned after the war, he went back to the Gazette and became Accounts Manager.

In the Gazette, he was quoted as saying, 'It's good to see old faces again. I'm glad everyone is well at home.'

Following in the tradition of several 137 members, his son played rugby for Fylde RUFC.

Other employees of the Gazette who served in the 137 and became POWs were E. Brown, H. Cockell, J. Cockcroft, I. Warde and K. Cusworth.

Leslie Haley

Tony Haley wrote to me about his father Leslie, a gunner with the 137.

Born in 1920, he died a relatively young man in 1972. At his inquest, the Coroner decided that his illness was due to the damage done to his body as a POW.

He was a plumber and was the first person to dive off the top board at Derby Baths, Blackpool in 1939. Prior to his death, he was a caretaker at Blackpool Town Hall.

Robert Hartley - Lieutenant

The story of Robert Hartley's death at Tebong is related in the main text of this book.

Robert was only 30 when he was killed. He was initially buried close to where he was killed and, after the war, re-buried at the British War Cemetery at Taiping.

My connection with Robert is through Fylde Rugby Club.

It was indeed a sobering moment for me, when I saw his name on the board listing past captains of the club. He, in 1935, with my own name some 32 years later.

Fylde Rugby Club's Captains' Board

George Irving Japp

George Irving Japp was born in Springburn, Glasgow in 1915. He became a wood worker and enlisted and joined the army in May 1938. He was posted to 137 and became a sergeant. He was amongst the first troops to be transported from Changi in June 1942 to Nong Pladuk. In 1944, he was moved back to Singapore to the River Valley Camp under the command of Lt Col. Eddie Gill. In February 1945, he was moved overseas to Camp 8 French Indo-China. In May 1945, he was moved again to Lianga Camp 10 in French Indo-China, and finally liberated on 12th September 1945. In due course, he returned to Blackpool and married his fiancée Nora Williamson. He died in October 2005.

William Leigh

Gunner William Leigh, originally from Hackney, as a POW had not been able to write a letter home to his parents throughout the period of his captivity, although he had sent six cards. His first letter dated 31 Aug 1945 was from Ubon POW camp in Thailand where he was working in the cookhouse and getting "fattened up" in preparation for his journey home.

He apologised for not being able to write, thanked his parents for writing to him, and told them that all their letters (and envelopes) had been used as cigarette papers. In his letters written on the voyage out to Malaya, he speaks of the heat of the cabins, so hot, in fact, that he along with many others slept on the bare boards of the deck. He speaks in wonder of sharks, porpoises and flying fish. He describes the evening entertainments of smoking and musical concerts, and the ceremony on crossing the Equator.

At one unnamed port of call, shore leave was permitted. Many of the troops were collected from the quayside by local residents, who entertained them for the period of leave. His letters were full of joyous amazement at a world he was seeing for the first time.

Harry Motteram

A native of Barrow, Harry's family moved to Blackpool in 1921, when Harry was just one year old.

They lived in Cromwell Road, Blackpool where Harry trained to be a plumber.

Early in 1939, he joined the Blackpool TA, eventually becoming part of the 137 Regiment and shipped out to Singapore.

Harry was a driver, undertaking the hard slog up to Jitra, and then the even harder journey back to Singapore and capture.

He was one of the original party sent from Changi up to Kanchanaburi. A succession of camps followed, including Tamarkan until his release in 1945

He sailed home from Rangoon on the *SS Orduna*, eventually arriving in Southampton weighing just six-and-a-half stone. He had five nights in camp in Southampton before travelling by train back to Blackpool.

On 30th March 2014. Harry gave an interview to Dr. Nigel Stanley .He talked of joining up, just to be one of the lads. He told of the rivalry between the batteries and the fact that they all had plenty of money as the lodgings allowance was very generous.

Whilst stationed in Liverpool, he was in charge of the water cart, which he had to test for impurities.

He relates his experiences at the battle of Slim River and tells how supportive the local Chinese population were.

He ended up fighting on the lawns of Raffles Hotel.

Harry enjoyed his time in Roberts Barracks and thought that imprisonment at Ban Pong was tolerable.

Whilst incarcerated, he suffered from malaria, and was operated on for appendicitis without an anaesthetic.

He thought the Korean guards were the most brutal, and he carried an intense dislike of the Japanese to his grave.

He resumed his occupation as a plumber, eventually dying in 2015.

At his death, he was the last surviving member of the 137.

Henry Newton

Henry, born in 1917 was a gunner from Doncaster. He was a butcher by trade (hence his nickname of 'Butch').

After capture in Singapore, he was sent Changi, then to Nong Pladuk followed by Konkoita, then back to Nong Pladuk 2 and finally back to Singapore River Valley Camp.

He was eventually transported on the hellship *Haruyasa Maru* to Saigon Group 10 Camp from where he was liberated on 12.09.45.

He became a postman after the war and eventually died in 1951.

Cary Owtram - Colonel

He lived at Newland Hall, Bay Horse, near Lancaster. He was married to Dorothy with a son Bob and two daughters, Jean and Patricia. Whilst in action, and before being captured, he had been promoted from the rank of Major to the rank of Colonel. He was made camp commander of Chungkai POW camp, the largest camp on the railway. His family did not know of his capture or his whereabouts for over a year.

In order to try and tackle the low prisoner morale in Chungkai, he established a police force, a hospital and a theatre. He was a talented tenor and often performed in the camp shows.

He was also instrumental in establishing the War Cemetery there, where there are 1426 Commonwealth and 313 Dutch War Graves.

On his return he brought back his diary which he had hidden in a bamboo pole before concealing it in a grave in Chungkai. He used the diary as the basis for his book '1000 days on the River Kwai'

He was awarded the OBE after the war.

A fellow prisoner wrote about him "on many occasions, I witnessed him receiving brutal beatings for his adamant and steadfast refusal to order sick men out to work on the Railway".

He died in 1993.

Leo Rawlings

Born in West Bromwich in 1918, he won a scholarship to the Central School of Art in Birmingham. Troubled by a speech defect, his naturally nervous sensitivity and the death of his mother, he achieved very little at the school and was removed at the request of the Headmaster.

His father relocated to Blackpool. Leo attended local art classes and passed every drawing and painting examination. By the time he was 17, he had his own business as a scenic and display artist. He joined the local TA, which is how he became a gunner in the 137.

His story as a serving member of the 137 is no different from the story of all the other members who were shipped to Malaya, and fought at Jitra and Slim River and who were eventually captured at the fall of Singapore.

Throughout his time as a POW he kept a pictorial record of his POW experiences which was concealed from the Japanese in a stove pipe under his bed.

In the 1950s and 60s, he drew comic strips for D.C. Thomson, The Victor and The Hornet among many others.

In 1972 an illustrated account of his experiences was published entitled, 'And the Dawn Came Up Like Thunder'.

His book was published in Japan by Takashi Nagase, whose encounters with another prisoner, Eric Lomax, is portrayed in Lomax's book, 'The Railwayman'.

Rawlings visited Nagase in 1980.

He died in 1990 and would no doubt have been amazed to learn the prices his paintings and drawing now fetch at auction.

The first photograph in his book shows Leo and three friends with whom he enlisted in 1939.

The picture shows Eric Newman, Clifford Davies and Bert Wright.

It is known that Bert Wright died on 6th February 1942 as a result of illness contracted during the retreat from the Battle of Slim River.

ROLL OF HONOUR 137TH FIELD REGIMENT RA

Officers			
37672	Lt Col	Holme	GD
71020	Captain	Liston	IFG
85529	Captain	Shore	JH
90351	Lieut	Moss	HS
903 57	Lieut	Storey	ID
153633	2nd Lieut	Hartley	R
95791	Lieut	Head	JA
Other Ranks			
1099744	Gunner	Alff	W
1097412	L/Bdr	Anstice	KH
944855	Sgt	Ashworth	G
932046	Gunner	Askew	R
1038788	L/Sgt	Baker	CH
948039	Gunner	Baker	J
1099745	Gunner	Baker	JH
944556	Gunner	Banks	W
1080671	Gunner	Barber	WJ
984118	Gunner	Barritt	F

1080674	Gunner	Barton	AF
1080677	Gunner	Baum	H
1115196	Gunner	Bayliss	AW
1099750	Gunner	Bond	AE
933105	Gunner	Bonney	W
779070	WO2 (BSM)	Boulter	JF
882432	L/Sgt	Bowker	WH
1034027	Bdr	Bowles	GF
902396	Gunner	Boyd	D
1080700	Gunner	Bridgeman	JH
2046058	Gunner	Brooks	JH
885149	Gunner	Brooks	KG
905035	Gunner	Broughton	R
950871	Gunner	Bullock	E
1080711	Gunner	Burns	EA
902561	Gunner	Burns	T
944576	Gunner	Burton	H
906315	Gunner	Butler	MJ
950893	Gunner	Cannell	CH
980542	Gunner	Capp	ON

199735	Gunner	Carne	A
930785	Gunner	Carter	CH
814460	L/Bdr	Cawthorne	W
950947	Gunner	Chadwick	WH
903546	Gunner	Challoner	D
833078	Gunner	Chambers	EA
952496	Gunner	Clark	RW
1099755	Gunner	Cohen	H
900410	Gunner	Cookson	F
930822	Gunner	Cooper	G
908416	Gunner	Cooper	KF
905040	L/Bdr	Crew	A
948091	Gunner	Crooke	G
896321	Gunner	Crossley	JA
890564	Gunner	Cuerdon	J
1099759	Gunner	Culpin	FW
931467	L/Bdr	Cumberbach	RE
1121226	Gunner	D'Arcy	CFJ
1097360	Gunner	Damon	AG
950856	Gunner	Davenport	AG

1116470	Gunner	Davies	SC
906307	W/Bdr	Death	WH
1080766	Gunner	Dellow	RV
906306	Gunner	Dennison	L
1080766	Gunner	Dixon	J
906305	Gunner	Donnelly	T
948033	Gunner	Donnelly	TP
1119461	Gunner	Doswell	EA
948053	Gunner	Dutson	HE
1119323	Gunner	Eaton	CA
905608	Gunner	Edge	H
1099764	Gunner	Esdell	RJ
1099765	Gunner	Ettridge	GAT
897910	Bdr	Foley	AE
845147	Gunner	Freak	GH
879032	Bdr	Frost	W
950943	Gunner	Garner	A
964784	Gunner	Hall	H
1099773	Gunner	Hall	WC
903543	Bdr	Hallworth	L

905089	Gunner	Hamer	CF
944557	Bdr	Hampson	GT
964719	Gunner	Hancock	FG
1099774	Gunner	Harding	AE
1080823	L/Bdr	Harmer	RC
930727	Gunner	Hayton	R
964234	Gunner	Hearnshaw	IA
896002	Gunner	Hirst	F
934135	Gunner	Hitchen	T
902535	Bdr	Holden	N
964796	Gunner	Hopkinson	E
896402	L/Bdr	Horsman	P
787517	WO2 (BSM)	Howarth	E
1096947	Gunner	Hoye	G
1099779	Gunner	Hughes	LH
950937	Gunner	Hume	T
916530	L/Sgt	Hurstfield	LA
1099781	Gunner	Jackson	HC
905587	Bdr	Jackson	JW
1099782	Gunner	Jacques	GW

950930	Gunner	Johnson	F
898809	Gunner	Johnson	J
1098440	Gunner	Jones	DB
948123	Bdr	Jones	EV
5104923	Sgt	Jones	G
950889	Gunner	Jones	TF
1110548	Gunner	Jones	TJ
1118052	Gunner	Keirle	FW
950917	Gunner	Kellett	AL
1108450	Gunner	Kelley	JL
950928	Gunner	Kendall	SD
113861	Gunner	Kennett	CM
1073700	Bdr	Key	FL
2578444	Sig	Kiernan	JA
950903	Gunner	King	E
921396	L/Bdr	Kirby	S
899370	Gunner	Lahey	J
1099785	Gunner	Lawrence	RA
944575	Gunner	Lee	F
1113517	Gunner	Leighton	J

950951	Bdr	Lingard	SJ
904404	Sgt	Little	E
964799	Gunner	Longbottom	W
905620	L/Sgt	Lumb	TG
1080893	Gunner	Macdonald	J
943857	Gunner	Machin	WE
948054	Gunner	Marland	E
908189	Sgt	Marshall	CN
1093566	Gunner	Martin	PL
906431	Gunner	Matthews	E
1116243	Gunner	May	ER
897908	Sgt	McKeowen	H
908192	Sgt	Meikle	E
950866	Gunner	Miller	A
998946	Gunner	Miller	AA
998946	Bdr	Miller	GG
905754	L/Bdr	Mitchell	IJ
889861	Gunner	Mitchell	JJW
948056	Gunner	Moon	D
951185	Gunner	Moore	G

933580	Gunner	Moran	J
998062	Gunner	Moreton	GEH
948037	Gunner	Morgan	HW
946716	Gunner	Morgan	J
895355	Sgt	Morrison	GD
119218	Gunner	Muffett	WH
823214	Gunner	Murphy	PT
960813	Gunner	Newby	L
908238	Sgt	Nicholas	P
949459	Gunner	Oakes	W
1119585	Gunner	Osmon	RF
964743	Gunner	Oxley	RF
953986	Gunner	Oxley	WE
909615	Gunner	Partridge	WJ
908200	Bdr	Parker	R
948048	L/Bdr	Parkinson	N
948058	Gunner	Parkinson	V
772650	WO11 (BSM)	Parkinson	W
961291	Gunner	Pearson	C
908195	Bdr	Pearson	R

950940	L/Bdr	Pendleton	W
800084	Gunner	Pitt	KW
900426	Gunner	Playforth	B
950933	Gunner	Preston	WK
1119330	Gunner	Price	LD
1099794	Gunner	Pullen	RGH
1099795	Gunner	Radley	FCW
2332286	Sgmn	Raymish	D
899328	Bdr	Reyknolds	LS
1080975	Gunner	Reynard	HE
885245	S/Sgt	Rice	TW
942246	Gunner	Ringer	WE
1080979	Gunner	Robbins	TH
781905	Gunner	Robinson	W
892044	Gunner	Robinson	WJ
950866	Bdr	Rogers	KD
908233	Gunner	Roscow	A
1119588	Gunner	Rowse	HA
1097287	Gunner	Russell	A
953987	Bdr	Salkeld	WE

908435	Gunner	Sanders	GA
895370	L/Bdr	Sanderson	W
1099797	Gunner	Saunders	JE
848138	Gunner	Seabridge	J
950935	Gunner	Sedgewick	L
1080994	Gunner	Seward	CW
892714	Gunner	Shenton	A
963913	Gunner	Sleney	EC
1113598	Gunner	Smith	CB
950883	L/Bdr	Smith	J
905531	Gunner	Southworth	JA
906298	L/Bdr	Spence	DA
908194	L/Sgt	Spencer	JB
964703	Gunner	Steele	L
1090613	Gunner	Stone	L
948110	Gunner	Stott	EH
948051	Gunner	Stringfellow	A
903393	Gunner	Stubbs	A
944578	Gunner	Sutcliffe	SA
1081756	Gunner	Taft	GE

1093633	Gunner	Takel	AJ
961459	Gunner	Taylor	E
895377	Gunner	Taylor	R
119334?	Gunner	Thomas	WD
948099	Gunner	Thompson	G
849754	Gunner	Tommany	J
906312	Gunner	Turnbull	J
902873?	L/Sgt	Waite	EN
1099803	Gunner	Waterman	D
1099804	Gunner	Webster	WH
948124	Gunner	West	F
1081788	Gunner	White	WW
1099805	Gunner	Whittle	S
906308	Bdr	Whitworh	A
924270	Gunner	Wilson	G
95074?	Gunner	Wood	J
1081807	L/Bdr	Woodward	EHW
1099807	Gunner	Wright	EE
907044	Gunner	Wright	H
1081814	Gunner	Wright	S

INDEX

DAVID TAYLOR

DAVID TAYLOR

ABOUT THE AUTHOR

David Taylor is a retired Solicitor. He lives in Lancashire.

In 2020, he self-published 'Beloved Ghosts, stories of Illawalla', the biggest bungalow in Europe and the Fylde Coast family who lived there.

www.ingramcontent.com/pod-product-compliance
Lightning Source LLC
Chambersburg PA
CBHW071610150726
48000CB00004B/1652